I0073435

Beyond the Fourteenth Amendment

ANASTASIA P. BODEN

Beyond the Fourteenth Amendment

PROTECTING THE
RIGHT TO EARN
A LIVING

Copyright © 2025 by the Cato Institute.
All rights reserved.
Cato Institute is a registered trademark.

Hardcover ISBN: 978-1-964524-87-0
eBook ISBN: 978-1-964524-88-7

Printed in the United States of America.

CATO INSTITUTE
1000 Massachusetts Ave. NW
Washington, DC 20001
www.cato.org

Table of Contents

Foreword. vii
Anastasia Boden

1. Defending Economic Liberty in State Courts: A Practitioner's Perspective 1
Timothy Sandefur

2. Unenumerated Stories: Tales of How Unenumerated Rights
Furthered Economic Liberty. 35
Anthony B. Sanders

3. Nondelegation and the Right to Earn a Living: An Untapped Opportunity 57
Ethan Blevins and Luke Wake

4. Protecting Economic Liberty under Both Article IV and
the Fourteenth Amendment. 87
Skylar Croy and Daniel P. Lennington

5. Overtaking the Gatekeepers: Antitrust Law as a Tool
to Break Up the Licensing Cartels. 117
Joshua Polk, Stephen Slivinski, and Caleb Trotter

6. Navigating the Economic Liberty Jurisprudence:
Lessons from Indian Legal Battles. 133
Prashant Narang

Foreword

By Anastasia Boden*

n January of 1872, a group of butchers came to the Supreme Court seeking to enforce the newly enacted Fourteenth Amendment and to reclaim their right to earn a living from the clutches of overeager government. The butchers argued that the state of Louisiana had granted favored interest groups a monopoly over butcher services, taking away their ability to put food on the table, and under the Fourteenth Amendment, they had a right to compete. Historians can argue about whether a monopoly was truly needed to remedy any sanitary issues of the time. But for the Supreme Court, whether the law was legitimate or simple economic protectionism didn't matter. As the Court has done so many times since, it effectively nullified a key part of that vastly important civil rights amendment and ruled that the Privileges or Immunities Clause only protects a very narrow set of rights that does not include the right to earn a living. It therefore left the precious right to channel one's passions and energies—to earn, to thrive, to make the world better, to provide for oneself or one's family, to find work in the occupation of one's choice—without any meaningful judicial protection and subject to the whims of legislative majorities.

Not much has changed in the 150 years since. In 2023, a woman from Louisiana who sought to provide care for special needs kids went to the Supreme Court asking the Justices to protect her right to enter her dream profession. There was no question that she was qualified, but Louisiana had denied her the ability to even seek licensure as a caregiver, on the theory that there were already enough caregivers and it didn't want to spend any time or money licensing anybody new. Because of *The Slaughter-House Cases*, and the Court's continued unwillingness to protect economic liberty under the Fourteenth Amendment, she was deprived of her dream, and Louisiana special needs children and their families were deprived of an important resource.

The effect of the Supreme Court's refusal to enforce the Fourteenth Amendment has been devastating. It's left a hole in civil rights law. Equality means nothing without the

* Anastasia Boden is a civil rights attorney at Pacific Legal Foundation. She was previously the director of the Robert A. Levy Center for Constitutional Studies at the Cato Institute.

right to move up the economic ladder and leave the circumstances of your birth. This legacy has left entrepreneurs of all kinds without any judicial recourse when the legislature keeps them out of a job. Physicians trying to work from home, hair braiders, taxi drivers, florists, household movers—many of them are left destitute, and their potential clients without options or with higher priced services, because courts offer no protection for the right to earn a living.

Though the courts keep telling us this is a policy dispute, we know there is no effective recourse in the legislature. We know that political minorities of all kinds, whether religious, racial, or ideological minorities (and of course, the smallest minority is the individual), cannot adequately protect themselves from the majority, and that's exactly why we have a Constitution and judicial review. There can be no individual rights without a judiciary to check executive or legislative overreach. And as courts have shied away from scrutinizing laws that restrict economic opportunity, licensing laws and other laws that make it difficult for people to get a job or to keep the fruits of their labor have metastasized.

But maybe it's not all the courts' fault. Maybe it's time for a moment of introspection—at least that's the premise of this journal. The vast majority of litigation aiming to restore the right to earn a living has been rooted in the Fourteenth Amendment, with litigators hoping that with better facts, more sympathetic plaintiffs, even more arbitrary laws, and even better lawyering, they can finally convince courts to take economic liberty seriously. But perhaps it's time to go beyond the Fourteenth Amendment. What can we, as lawyers, researchers, academics, policy wonks, pundits, or people who care about entrepreneurship and innovation, do to restore the right to earn a living once we look to *other* parts of the Constitution?

The aim of this journal is to consider new strategies for reviving the precious, and undoubtedly fundamental, right to earn a living. It is the authors' hope that one day, one of these theories makes its way back to the Supreme Court and accomplishes what litigation under the Fourteenth Amendment has been unable to do. We hope litigators will use these theories as a blueprint to make real change in the law.

The first two pieces urge supporters of economic freedom to look at state constitutions. In the first, Timothy Sandefur recaps challenges and opportunities for litigating in state courts. He tells us that, contrary to how most of us understand federal constitutional practice, "in doing state constitutional law, one begins not with the text, but with the history." That is, "the practitioner must first know how many state constitutions there have been, when and under what circumstances they were written, and what materials are available for research." This makes litigation, at least in some ways, more challenging. But it also means there is significant opportunity for attorneys to become experts in underexplored fields.

In our second article, Anthony Sanders looks at the myriad provisions protecting unenumerated rights in state constitutions to argue that when judges protect the right to earn a living, they're not "making stuff up." Rather, they're "enforcing constitutional text." He recounts various cases throughout history where judges have applied state constitutions to protect people from abusive government, and contrary to what government lawyers threatened, the heavens did not fall. Instead, entrepreneurs were allowed to pursue livelihoods free from irrational interference and government continued to enforce its valid health and safety regulations that were on the books.

Next, Ethan Blevins and Luke Wake consider whether crony occupational licensing boards are subject to litigation under the nondelegation doctrine. State licensing statutes often delegate "capacious authority" for boards to decide questions that completely disrupt people's ability to enter an occupation, including "who qualifies for a license, what restrictions apply for licensed individuals, and what the scope of a licensed practice is." Many times, "the statutes provide no governing standards at all," which conflicts with the foundational principle that legislators, not unaccountable bureaucrats, are tasked with passing laws.

Next, Skylar Croy and Daniel Lennington evaluate the Privileges and Immunities Clause of Article IV in order to present evidence that the Supreme Court has misinterpreted the Privileges or Immunities Clause of the Fourteenth Amendment. The authors suggest bringing more cases under Article IV "to confront th[e] fundamental question" of why "a 'privilege' or 'immunity' clearly protected by Article IV" is *not* always treated as a "privilege" or "immunity" protected under the Fourteenth Amendment.

In the penultimate article, Joshua Polk, Stephen Slivinski, and Caleb Trotter suggest that antitrust should be weaponized against anti-competitive licensing bodies, which are often comprised of members of the regulating trade and therefore pass regulations in their own interest rather than the interest of the public at large. The Supreme Court has shown some sympathy toward using antitrust laws against the "greatest perpetrators of anticompetitive conduct," regulatory boards captured by self-interest.

In the final article, Dr. Prashant Narang parses the last decade of economic liberty litigation in India for insights into how to effectively protect entrepreneurship in the United States. He finds fascinating parallels between cronyism in India and in the United States, and he suggests that courts are more sympathetic to economic liberty when attorneys can show alignment with sympathetic third-party interests.

The Center for Constitutional Studies hopes that readers will walk away believing that there's hope yet for the constitutional right to earn a living—and be inspired to help lead the charge.

Defending Economic Liberty in State Courts: A Practitioner's Perspective

By Timothy Sandefur*

INTRODUCTION

The past two decades have seen extraordinary progress in promoting constitutional protections for the neglected right to earn a living. Much of that progress has been made under the banner of the Fourteenth Amendment.[1] But much remains to be done, particularly through litigation in state court, under state constitutions.[2] Cases such as *Raffensperger v. Jackson*,[3] *Coleman v. City of Mesa*,[4] and *Ladd v. Real Estate Commission*[5] indicate that state judges may be more likely, at least in some circumstances, to meaningfully protect economic freedom against unjustifiable intrusion than are their federal colleagues. In part, this is due to prevailing attitudes about the role of federal courts, particularly the notion that they should be passive (or "restrained"), rather than "activist." But it is also due to the fact that state constitutions typically contain more explicit protections for property rights and economic freedom than does the federal constitution. The political and constitutional histories of states also tend to shed

* Timothy Sandefur is the Vice President for Legal Affairs at the Goldwater Institute, and holds the 2022–23 Barry M. Goldwater Chair in American Institutions, Arizona State University.

1. I review that progress and offer thoughts on issues to be addressed in the future in *Rebuilding the Fourteenth Amendment: The Prospects and the Pitfalls*, 12 N.Y.U. J.L. & LIBERTY 278 (2019).

2. *See generally* Clint Bolick, *State Constitutions: Freedom's Frontier*, 2016–17 CATO SUP. CT. REV. 15.

3. 888 S.E.2d 483 (Ga. 2023).

4. 284 P.3d 863 (Ariz. 2012).

5. 230 A.3d 1096 (Pa. 2020).

greater light on the importance of protecting economic freedom of choice, offering greater argumentative warrant for those inclined to protect economic freedom against unjustifiable state interference.

Because I approach this subject as a practitioner rather than an academic, I wish to explore here some of the routes that remain to be explored by those litigating in defense of the right to earn a living under state constitutions. I begin with some observations on the practice of state constitutional law—its challenges and benefits—and follow that with some suggestions regarding specific issues that state courts must address if we are to restore the right to earn a living to its proper place alongside other constitutionally protected freedoms.

I. DOING STATE CONSTITUTIONAL LAW

A. The Challenges and Opportunities

It's almost a cliché now that state constitutions offer greater opportunities for protection of individual freedom than the federal constitution does.[6] Yet this path still remains insufficiently explored by litigators. And state courts, even when presented with state constitutional arguments, still sometimes choose to disregard them and to follow a "lock-step" approach instead, parroting federal legal theories when interpreting their own constitutions.[7]

What accounts for this blind spot? There are several, overlapping answers. For one thing, political pressures may cause state judges to resist deviating from federal jurisprudential theories.[8] Of course, in some contexts, contrary pressures can embolden them to do so. But even if we confine ourselves to legal considerations, there may be several reasons why judges and lawyers resist taking advantage of state constitutionalism. For one thing, our legal education system tends to exaggerate the importance of the federal constitution at the expense of state constitutions. Most law students are required to take a class in federal constitutional law, whereas the typical law school offers perhaps a

---

6. *See, e.g.*, Jeffrey Sutton, 51 IMPERFECT SOLUTIONS: STATES AND THE MAKING OF AMERICAN CONSTITUTIONAL LAW (2018); William J. Brennan, Jr., *State Constitutions and the Protection of Individual Rights*, 90 HARV. L. REV. 489 (1977).

7. For a particularly egregious example, see State v. Mixton, 478 P.3d 1227 (Ariz. 2021).

8. This is particularly true with respect to criminal justice matters. *See* Timothy Sandefur, *The Arizona "Private Affairs" Clause*, 51 ARIZ. ST. L.J. 723, 767–72 (2019).

single, elective course in state constitutional law. Law professors, who generate most of our constitutional scholarship, also have a far greater incentive to focus on federal rather than state constitutional law. Becoming a specialist on one of the amendments in the federal bill of rights is likely to bring many professional rewards and even make one a celebrity, whereas becoming the nation's foremost expert on the Rhode Island Constitution's "rights of fishery" clause[9] probably won't.

Then there's the challenge of mastering the material. State constitutions are usually much longer than the federal constitution and change with much greater rapidity, which makes it harder to become familiar with their nuances, and there is vastly more archival material to be sifted through when engaging in state constitutional law than when engaging in federal constitutional law. A lawyer seeking to make an originalist argument about the federal constitution might consult *The Federalist* and *The Antifederalist*, the debates at the Philadelphia Constitutional Convention and the ratification conventions, and perhaps a few eighteenth-century dictionaries and newspaper articles. She will also have the assistance of extensive scholarship by the nation's top legal scholars.

By contrast, a lawyer seeking to make an originalist argument about, say, the Texas Constitution, will have to examine the debates and writings concerning the constitutions of 1827, 1836, 1845, 1861, 1866, and 1869, in addition to dictionaries and newspapers covering these eras, and be familiar with important developments in Texas history that might be relevant to understanding these texts. A lawyer in a state that was a territory prior to statehood will have to consider federal statutes governing the territories before the state's admission, too. Lawyers in states with the initiative process may have to research ballot pamphlets from important historical elections. Lawyers in Missouri and some other states must confront the fact that there are no recorded debates from some of their state constitutional conventions, and more recently, state constitutions (Georgia's, for example) have been written not by conventions but by special commissions dedicated to that purpose; an attorney may have to comb through those reports, too. Records of some state constitutional conventions are spotty and incomplete.[10] Some records are simply inaccessible. The debates at Montana's 1884 constitutional

---

9. R.I. CONST. art. I, § 17.

10. The records of Arizona's 1910 constitutional convention were published only in 1991, and despite the heroic work of editor John S. Goff, they still contain many lacunae. *See* JOHN S. GOFF, ED., THE RECORDS OF THE ARIZONA CONSTITUTIONAL CONVENTION OF 1910 (1991). Also, the delegates at the Arizona

convention were recorded but never transcribed and remain almost entirely in hand-written form.[11] Few historians have studied these conventions in much depth, meaning the practitioner is likely to find herself the first person ever to have researched whatever constitutional question she is pursuing.[12]

All of this makes for both a challenge and an opportunity for anyone seeking to offer a state constitutional argument. It also ensures a wide field of research projects for future legal scholars.

One reason this enterprise holds so much promise is that states typically have remark-ably rich legal traditions and experiences. State constitutions reflect challenges that were faced, and reforms that were adopted, in the generations that followed the federal constitution. State constitutional gift clauses, for example, which prohibit giving or lend-ing money or credit to private enterprises, all postdate the U.S. Constitution and reflect the disastrous experiences resulting from nineteenth-century government subsidies to railroad and canal companies.[13] The same is true of the special law clauses of state con-stitutions, which bar legislatures from granting particular privileges to specific groups,[14] and the eminent domain provisions of several state constitutions, which are more spe-cific than the federal Fifth Amendment in prohibiting private takings.[15]

It should go without saying that not only *may* state courts interpret their state consti-tutions without relying on the federal courts' interpretation of the federal constitution (as long as they do not interpret them as less protective of individual rights), but it's pos-itively irrational for them to do otherwise, in many cases. Obviously, where a state con-stitutional provision uses wholly different language from the analogous provision in the federal constitution, there's no colorable argument for interpreting the former in

convention, like those in many other states, did most of their substantive work in committee, the debates of which were never recorded.

11. They are now available at https://scholarworks.umt.edu/montanaconstitution/2/.

12. California's constitution, for example, was written at a convention in 1878–79. Only one book has ever been published about that convention: CARL BRENT SWISHER, MOTIVATION AND POLITICAL TECHNIQUE IN THE CALIFORNIA CONSTITUTIONAL CONVENTION 1878–79 (1930). It is 132 pages long.

13. *See generally* Timothy Sandefur, *The Origins of the Arizona Gift Clause*, 36 REGENT U. L. REV. 1 (2024).

14. *See, e.g.*, ARIZ. CONST. art. IV, pt. 2, § 19.

15. *See, e.g.*, WASH. CONST. art. I, § 16.

"lockstep" with the latter.[16] But even where the language of the federal and state constitutions is identical, this provides no justification for a state court to simply follow the federal courts' interpretation of the federal constitution—especially where that federal interpretation *postdates* the state constitution. And there may be other historical, political, and cultural factors that justify a state court interpreting their constitution's language differently.[17]

These considerations are complicated by the fact that some state constitutions contain multiple overlapping provisions of similar or even identical wording: the New York and Arkansas Constitutions, for example, contain both "law of the land" and "due process" clauses,[18] even though these phrases have long been viewed as synonymous. Even if "lockstep" interpretation were warranted in some cases, it's impossible to see how it would apply here.

Historically speaking, it ought to be federal courts that follow state constitutional doctrines, not vice versa. Some state constitutions are older than the federal version, or contain provisions that are older, and federal courts have often modeled their jurisprudence on state legal theories. A lawyer who today looks through the cases may be misled into thinking that federal courts originated these doctrines. Take the law of just compensation, for example, which did not reach the federal courts in any significant way until *Chicago B. & Q. Railroad v. Chicago*,[19] a century after the earliest state cases addressing compensation for damage to property. Even today, the Supreme Court will often survey how state courts have addressed some constitutional controversy before pronouncing its own doctrine.[20] And, in fact, state courts have often developed rich bodies of law addressing a variety of subjects before federal courts have encountered those questions. State constitutional litigation has often proven, so to speak, to be the ground floor

---

16. *But see Mixton*, 478 P.3d 1227 (Ariz. 2021).

17. Rachel A. Van Cleave, *State Constitutional Interpretation and Methodology*, 28 N.M. L. REV. 199, 203 (1998). *See further* Ravin v. State, 537 P.2d 494 (Alaska, 1975) (holding, based on state culture, that Alaska's constitutional privacy guarantee includes a right to consume marijuana in the privacy of one's home).

18. *See* N.Y. CONST. art. I, §§ 1, 6; ARK. CONST. art. II, §§ 8, 21.

19. 166 U.S. 226 (1897).

20. *See generally* Steven G. Calabresi, et al., *The U.S. and the State Constitutions: An Unnoticed Dialogue*, 9 N.Y.U. J. L. & LIBERTY 685 (2015).

in the development of federal legal doctrine. It is foolhardy, therefore, to assume the federal-primacy stance that often permeates the discourse of constitutional law.

In doing state constitutional law, one begins not with the text, but with the history.[21] The practitioner must first know how many state constitutions there have been,[22] when and under what circumstances they were written, and what materials are available for research.[23] The text of a state constitutional provision may have been copied from an earlier version into a later version, or from another state's constitution, so the researcher will probably have to consult the records of more than one state constitutional convention. These borrowings sometimes result in a change of wording, and state constitutional revision commissions have sometimes altered the wording of certain clauses. Thus, for example, the California Constitution's provisions relating to eminent domain, which now read, "Private property may be taken or damaged for a public use and only when just compensation, ascertained by a jury unless waived, has first been paid to, or into court for, the owner,"[24] is a modernization of language that appeared in the 1879 constitution, which declared, "Private property shall not be taken or damaged for public use without just compensation having been first made to, or paid into Court for, the owner. . . ."[25] That modernization was the work of the state's constitutional revision commission in the 1970s, and no change in meaning resulted from it—but the 1879 language was adapted with changes from the language of the 1849 constitution, which had been copied from the Fifth Amendment to the federal constitution: "nor shall private property be taken for public use without just compensation."[26] The 1879 alterations *did* change the meaning; they were added after experience with the abusive practices of railroad development,

---

21. "[T]hose interpreting state constitutions must be prepared to act as constitutional geologists, examining the textual layers from various eras in order to arrive at their interpretations." G. Alan Tarr, *Interpreting the Separation of Powers in State Constitutions*, 59 N.Y.U. ANN. SURV. AM. L. 329, 332 (2003).

22. A helpful list of them can be found in JOHN J. DINAN, THE AMERICAN STATE CONSTITUTIONAL TRADITION 8–9 (2006).

23. A list of extant state convention debate records can be found in *id.* at 279–85.

24. CAL. CONST. art. I, § 19(a).

25. CAL. CONST. art. I, § 14 (1879).

26. CAL. CONST. art. I, § 8 (1849).

which often deprived people of property unjustly.[27] This is just one example of why the practitioner engaged in state constitutional law must be attentive to variations in wording and their possible implications (or lack thereof).

One must also attend to the possible interactions between different state constitutional clauses, which may have implications for interpretation. For example, the Arizona Constitution's "private affairs" clause[28] prohibits the state from intruding into the "private affairs" of any person. But the state's corporations commission, which enjoys its own article in the state constitution, is elsewhere authorized to inspect the "books, papers, business methods, and affairs" of corporations,[29] and another provision of the constitution requires certain types of businesses to keep their records available "at all times" for the "visitorial and inquisitorial powers of the state, *notwithstanding the immunities and privileges secured in the declaration of rights of this Constitution.*"[30] The italicized phrase indicates that the authors of these clauses were aware of the possible tension between them, which gives rise to the inference (per the *exclusio alterius* rule) that except for those records that must be made available at all times for state examination, the private affairs clause bars the state from demanding to see a person's financial information absent "lawful authority."[31] Or consider the Arizona gift clause's prohibition on the state giving "aid" to private enterprises "by subsidy or otherwise."[32] Does this forbid the state from granting tax exemptions to private firms as incentives to development? The answer is likely to be found by comparing this clause with another clause, which forbids the state from making appropriations "in aid of" any church.[33] The latter clause does not contain the phrase "by subsidy or otherwise," which implies that it's less absolute than the prohibition on "aid" to private enterprises—and,

27. *See generally* Timothy Sandefur, *A Natural Rights Perspective on Eminent Domain in California: A Rationale for Meaningful Judicial Scrutiny of "Public Use,"* 32 SW. U. L. REV. 569, 573–653 (2003).

28. ARIZ. CONST. art. II, § 8.

29. ARIZ. CONST. art. XV, § 4.

30. ARIZ. CONST. art. XIV, § 16 (emphasis added).

31. *See further* Sandefur, *"Private Affairs" Clause, supra* note 8 at 736.

32. ARIZ. CONST. art. IX, § 7.

33. ARIZ. CONST. art. IX, § 10.

consequently, that the phrase "by subsidy or otherwise" was intended, *inter alia*, to ban tax-exemption subsidies.[34]

Such "holistic" interpretation is commonplace in federal constitutional law, but given the greater complexity of state constitutional law, it is particularly important to bear it in mind here. It can sometimes be complicated—consider, for example, the fact that Missouri's constitution has four separate provisions governing the use of eminent domain for redevelopment, adopted at various times.[35] One, which appeared in the state's initial constitution in 1820, permits takings for "public use."[36] Another, which first appeared in the 1875 constitution, expressly forbids takings for "private use."[37] Still another, which was adopted at the 1945 constitutional convention, allows takings for purposes of "rehabilitation of blighted, substandard, or insanitary areas."[38] Yet it is the task of the lawyer and judge to reconcile these texts.

The practitioner should also be attentive to incidents in state history that may be relevant to the meaning of a state constitutional provision. Arizona's gift clause provides a striking example.[39] This provision is the strongest prohibition on state subsidization of industry in the country. It was copied verbatim from the Montana Constitution of 1879. The wording is particularly strong because both states, during their territorial days, engaged in irresponsible subsidization of businesses, especially railroads, leading to financial catastrophe. Among other things, Arizona Territory subsidized construction of a railroad in Pima County, which proved almost farcical in its failure.[40] Disputes over its legality reached the U.S. Supreme Court,[41] and this misadventure, along with others in

---

34. *See* Kotterman v. Killian, 972 P.2d 606, 621 (Ariz. 1999). *See further* Timothy Sandefur, *The Arizona Gift Clause in the Twenty-First Century*, 16 DREXEL L. REV. 299 (2024).

35. MO. CONST. art. I, §§ 26–28; art. VI, § 21.

36. MO. CONST. art. I, § 26. This appeared as Article I, Section 7 of the 1820 Constitution. Its language was modified slightly and placed in Article I, Section 16 of the 1865 Constitution.

37. MO. CONST. art. I, § 28. In the 1875 Constitution, this appeared, in slightly different wording, in Article II, Section 20.

38. MO. CONST. art. IV, § 21.

39. *See generally* Sandefur, *Origins, supra* note 13.

40. *See generally* Howard A. Hubbard, *A Chapter in Early Arizona Transportation History: The Arizona Narrow Gauge Railroad Company*, 5 U. ARIZ. BULL. 1 (1934).

41. Lewis v. Pima County, 155 U.S. 54 (1894).

Prescott and elsewhere, led to Arizona being denied admission to the Union in 1891. When the territory tried again, in 1910, it did so under a constitution that included an extraordinarily strong prohibition on government subsidies to private businesses. This episode helps shed light on the goals the clause was intended to accomplish.

An important source for practitioners of state constitutional law is period newspapers and magazines. These can provide invaluable information on legal and constitutional precedents—information often omitted from official records. For example, one recent Arizona Supreme Court case concerned the rules governing petition circulation for ballot initiatives;[42] the state constitution requires actual, in-person, pen-and-ink signatures.[43] The question presented in the case was whether, in light of the COVID-19 pandemic, this requirement could be waived and an online alternative employed. In arguing the case, it was helpful to consult newspapers from 1918 to determine how the state had coped with the influenza epidemic a century earlier.[44]

It is not only a state's own historical development that plays a role in understanding a state constitutional provision; other states' histories can also be relevant, given that the authors of state constitutions have sometimes borrowed language from each other, or have drafted language specifically to avoid what they view as inadequacies in other states. One of the great political controversies of the nineteenth century involved tax exemptions as a form of subsidy. In the 1850s, Illinois legislators granted the Illinois Central an exemption from taxes in order to encourage railroad development. By 1907, it became clear that the company had never paid a dime in taxes, or so critics charged. Thus the authors of the Arizona Constitution in 1910 likely had this type of abuse in mind when fashioning the state's prohibition on subsidies.[45]

Practitioners engaged in state constitutional law should take care to spot terms of art that might indicate influences in state constitutional development. For example, the 1879 California Constitution employed phrases such as "affected with a public interest" in many clauses, and did so in response to the U.S. Supreme Court's decision in *Munn v.*

---

42. Arizonans for Second Chances, Rehab., & Pub. Safety v. Hobbs, 471 P.3d 607 (Ariz. 2020).

43. ARIZ. CONST. art. IV, pt. 1, § 9.

44. *See* Brief Amicus Curiae of Goldwater Institute, et al., Arizonans for Second Chances v. Hobbs, No. CV-20-0098-SA, https://www.goldwaterinstitute.org/wp-content/uploads/2020/04/Second-Chances-Brief .pdf.

45. *See* Sandefur, *Origins, supra* note 13 at 33–38, 53–54.

Illinois,[46] which established the "affected with a public interest test," precursor to the rational basis test. Previous generations were prone to using clichés and slogans in political debate as much as we are, and practitioners should keep an eye out for the tendency of constitutional drafters and judges to speak in legal and literary allusions. For example, the phrase "persons capable of becoming citizens of the United States" was employed in the nineteenth century as a polite euphemism for excluding Chinese immigrants, who at the time were barred from citizenship.[47] One often encounters this phrase in nineteenth-century political debates, both in newspapers and at the 1878–79 constitutional convention.

The practitioner should also be aware of the incentives faced by state court judges. Judges will naturally seek reassurance that staking out a jurisprudence that differs from federal law is not only warranted as a doctrinal matter, but will also not lead to bad consequences. In *State v. Gunwall,*[48] the Washington Supreme Court offered a test for determining when a state court should interpret its state constitution without reliance on federal doctrine. Other courts have offered similar tests.[49] One might observe that even having such a test illogically shifts the burden to the wrong side: state courts should begin with the presumption of relying on state law, and only consult federal law when required to. But in any event, the practitioner who asks a state court to step out from under the shield of federal doctrine must be prepared to address pragmatic as well as doctrinal concerns about doing so.[50] A lawyer making a state constitutional argument

46. 94 U.S. (4 Otto) 113 (1876).

47. *See, e.g.,* Spring Val. Water Works v. Bd. of Sup'rs of City & Cnty. of San Francisco, 61 Cal. 18, 39 (1882) (McKinstry, J., dissenting) (decrying a decision which he believed made it impossible for a city "to require that the organizers of a water corporation shall be citizens, or persons capable of becoming citizens.").

48. 720 P.2d 808, 812–13 (Wash. 1986).

49. *See, e.g.,* People v. Caballes, 851 N.E.2d 26 (Ill. 2006); State v. Hunt, 450 A.2d 952, 965–67 (N.J. 1982) (Handler, J., concurring); Commonwealth v. Edmunds, 586 A.2d 887, 895 (Pa. 1991).

50. One is reminded here of Friedrich Nietzsche's reflection on the difference between "free spirits" and "bound spirits." FRIEDRICH NIETZSCHE, HUMAN, ALL TOO HUMAN 139–42 (Marian Faber & Stephen Lehmann trans., University of Nebraska Press, 1996) (1878). Free spirits, he wrote, "demand[] reasons, while others demand faith"—whereas bound spirits blindly follow tradition and think that "all things that benefit [them] are in the right." *Id.* at 142. Consequently, whenever free spirits find themselves "pleading their cause before the tribunal of bound spirits," they can only win their cases if they "prove that there have always been free spirits and that freethinking therefore has permanence; then, that they do not want to be a burden; and finally, that on the whole they are beneficial to bound spirits." *Id.*

will probably be working with a blank slate, and should be prepared to offer some sort of test that will demonstrate to the court that ruling in her favor will not cause political or economic havoc. It tends to be in the state government's interest—and state courts' interest, too—for state courts to interpret a state's constitution in "lockstep" with the federal constitution, simply because doing so demands less of officials, administrators, and the government's lawyers. The practitioner must be prepared to assuage these concerns.

B. The Turn to Natural Law Reasoning

State courts have had to address "all the objects which, in the ordinary course of affairs, concern the lives, liberties, and properties of the people, and the internal order, improvement, and prosperity of the State."[51] They have declared, for example, that occupational licensing laws prohibiting people from practicing photography without a license are irrational under their state constitutions.[52] They have declared protectionist laws regulating food sales illegitimately discriminatory under their state constitutions.[53] And they have repeatedly refused to follow the federal "anything goes" version of the rational basis test, insisting that while the state has broad discretion to regulate economic matters, that discretion must actually be reasonable, rather than being predicated on wholly imaginary rationalizations.[54] State constitutional litigation thus offers many opportunities, but demands consideration of unique factors.

One positive development in this respect is that in the wake of the U.S. Supreme Court's *Dobbs* decision,[55] state courts have been forced to break new state constitutional ground, whether they want to or not. This will certainly prove healthy for constitutional discourse. Consider the extraordinarily well reasoned decisions in *Hodes & Nauser, MDs, P.A.*

---

51. THE FEDERALIST No. 45 at ___ (J. Cooke, ed., 1961) (James Madison).

52. *See* Buehman v. Bechtel, 114 P.2d 227 (Ariz. 1941), and cases cited therein. *See further* Paul Avelar & Keith Diggs, *Economic Liberty and the Arizona Constitution: A Survey of Forgotten History*, 49 ARIZ. ST. L.J. 355 (2017).

53. *See, e.g.*, Moultrie Milk Shed v. City of Cairo, 57 S.E.2d 199 (Ga. 1950).

54. *See, e.g.*, Patel v. Texas Dep't of Licensing & Regul., 469 S.W.3d 69 (Tex. 2015); *Ladd*, 230 A.3d at 1108; *Raffensperger*, 888 S.E.2d at 492.

55. Dobbs v. Jackson Women's Health Organization, 142 S. Ct. 2228 (2022).

v. Schmidt,[56] *Medical Licensing Board v. Planned Parenthood,*[57] and *Planned Parenthood Great Nw. v. State.*[58] Whatever one thinks of abortion rights, these decisions mark fine exercises in constitutional reasoning, which do not shy away from the demands of natural law legal philosophy. This is likely to have beneficial consequences for economic liberty jurisprudence, both because economic liberty is logically inextricable from "personal" liberty, and because decisions on questions of natural rights help habituate state courts to taking the so-called countermajoritarian stance. The Indiana Supreme Court, for example, acknowledged in *Planned Parenthood* that the state constitution's protections for individual rights are premised on the idea that each person has an inherent freedom which "include[s] natural rights" such as the "property" everyone has in his or her own person and labor.[59] Thus the constitution protects "unenumerated rights," the court said, including "pursuing a vocation that does not harm others."[60]

What these decisions teach is that when state courts undertake their duty to independently apply their own state constitutions, they *are* competent both to weigh the philosophical issues that judges are obligated to resolve and to consider the lessons of their own state constitutional histories, in order to address important questions about the nature and boundaries of individual rights. The materials are there, and the judges can do the work. The next question is, will *we?*

II. FUTURE PATHS FOR THE PROTECTION OF ECONOMIC FREEDOM

State constitutions contain many provisions that are either wholly absent from the federal constitution or are phrased differently than in it, often specifically for the purpose of providing greater protection than the federal constitution does. Some of these are "positive rights" provisions, such as those guaranteeing a right to an education,[61] which are legacies of the Populist and Progressive Eras. Between 1875 and 1900, 26 of the then 45

---

56. 440 P.3d 461 (Kan. 2019).

57. 211 N.E.3d 957 (Ind. 2023).

58. 522 P.3d 1132 (Idaho 2023).

59. 211 N.E.3d at 967.

60. *Id.* at 968–69.

61. *See, e.g.*, W. VA. CONST. art. XII, § 1; ARIZ. CONST. art. XI, § 1.

states held constitutional conventions, and some held more than one, making this the most productive constitution-making period in American history. But constitution makers during this era were also concerned with the overreaching of government power, and most of the distinctive provisions of state constitutions involve "negative rights"— that is, restrictions on government power intended to protect against abuses that were only encountered in the decades following ratification of the U.S. Constitution. These include the protections against eminent domain and subsidies that I have mentioned, which were adopted after experience with railroad expansion. These and other provisions offer unique opportunities for protecting the rights of entrepreneurship.

A. Fruits of One's Labor Clauses

North Carolina,[62] Missouri,[63] Oklahoma,[64] and likely other states[65] constitutionally guarantee the individual's right to the "fruits of his or her own labor," or some variation on this phrase. This clearly contemplates the right to engage in exchange for one's own economic betterment and to enjoy the benefit.

Consider North Carolina. In *Kinsley v. Ace Speedway Racing*,[66] the owners of an automobile racetrack challenged the constitutionality of the governor's orders commanding them to cease operations in light of the COVID-19 pandemic. They argued that the governor allowed other, competing racetracks to operate, and that they were singled out by the governor as a result of the owner's criticism of the governor's actions.[67] They further argued that the state's actions violated the state's "fruits of one's labor" clause. The court of appeals allowed the case to proceed, explaining that this clause was intended to

---

62. N.C. CONST. art. I, § 1.

63. MO. CONST. art. I, § 2. An excellent starting point for research on Missouri's clause is David Roland's opening brief in Missouri Veterinary Med. Bd. v. Gray, 2012 WL 5338469, **38–41.

64. OKLA. CONST. art. II, § 2.

65. The Maryland Constitution of 1865 expressly protected this right as well. *See* MD. CONST. art. § I (1864) (protecting "the enjoyment of the proceeds of their own labor."). Although it is omitted from the current version of Maryland's Constitution, drafted in 1867, the 1867 constitution specifies that "this enumeration of Rights shall not be construed to impair or deny others retained by the People." MD. CONST. art. 45. It would be unreasonable to doubt that among the "other" rights retained by this provision are those specified in earlier versions of the state constitution.

66. 877 S.E. 2d 54 (N.C. App. 2022), review allowed, 883 S.E.2d 455 (N.C. 2023).

67. *Id.* at 67.

"increase the floor of protections granted by similar provisions in the United States federal constitution," and to guarantee "North Carolina citizens' . . . 'right to earn a living' in whatever occupation they desire[]."[68] While the state may regulate in order to protect the public against dishonest or dangerous activities, "this clause applies when our government, most often the legislature, enacts a scheme of legislation or regulation that purports to protect the public from undesirable actors within occupations."[69] (At the time of writing, this case is still on appeal.)

Missouri courts have been less receptive to "fruits of one's labor" arguments. However, in *Fisher v. State Highway Commission* in 1997, the state supreme court remarked that the clause was drafted with an eye to slavery, and that, with one exception, it had only been enforced against state actions that compelled people to labor without compensation.[70] Since *Fisher*, state courts have taken a deferential approach. In a 2013 "fruits of one's labor" case, the Missouri Court of Appeals upheld the constitutionality of requiring people who "float" horses' teeth to obtain a veterinary license, despite the fact that they do not engage in veterinary medicine, on the grounds that "when the legislature has spoken on the subject, the courts must defer to its determinations of public policy."[71] Such deference disregards the legal history of the clause, which includes significant protections for economic freedom. In 1910, the court found that a maximum-hours law—similar to that at issue in *Lochner v. New York*[72]—was invalid under the "fruits of one's labor" clause.[73] Two years later, the court found a law unconstitutional which prohibited students in barber colleges from charging money for haircuts while they were still in school.[74] There is no foundation for judicial deference here. The Missouri Supreme

68. *Id.* at 61.

69. *Id.* at 62.

70. 948 S.W.2d 607, 610 (Mo. 1997).

71. Missouri Veterinary Med. Bd. v. Gray, 397 S.W.3d 479, 482–83 (Mo. Ct. App. 2013) (quoting Budding v. SSM Healthcare System, 19 S.W.3d 678, 682 (Mo. banc 2000)).

72. 198 U.S. 45 (1905).

73. State v. Miksicek, 125 S.W. 507, 508 (Mo. 1910). Notably, the act in question applied only to bakeries that produced biscuits, bread, or cakes, and did not apply to bakeries that produced pies, pastries, or crackers. *Id.* at 511. The court also found this discrimination to violate the state constitution's prohibition on special privileges. *Id.*

74. Moler v. Whisman, 147 S.W. 985 (Mo. 1912).

Court's employment of deference doctrines—themselves hand-me-downs from federal jurisprudence—shows how far we still have to go.

Oklahoma courts, too, have held that their "fruits of one's labor" clause allows the state to regulate business activities in order to protect "public order, safety, health, morals and the general welfare of society,"[75] and some cases have viewed this with excessive leniency toward the government. In a 1998 case, for example, an Oklahoma court held that a state law prohibiting people from selling coffins without first obtaining a funeral director's license was constitutional under this clause, because caskets are "part of the funeral service business"[76]—a stunningly superficial analysis typical of judicial deference.

But such decisions should not deter litigators from concentrating their efforts on fashioning a "fruits of one's labor" jurisprudence. These clauses have been underutilized and underresearched. In fact, there appears to be no significant scholarship published on the origin and scope of these clauses. It is no surprise, then, that judges would find it difficult to envision a ruling that takes full advantage of this clause.

It is not that the materials are lacking. The *Fisher* court was right that they were drafted in the wake of the Civil War, in light of the "free labor" philosophy[77] that underlay the anti-slavery movement, as was the Fourteenth Amendment. But just as that amendment is concerned not solely with slavery, so the "fruits of one's labor" clauses focus on an underlying evil of which chattel slavery was but one manifestation. One of the chief moral objections to slavery is that it violates the inherent right that each person has to devote his or her skills to making a living. The individual owns him- or herself, and his or her own labor. This cannot be justly forbidden or transferred to another.[78] To deprive

75. Edmondson v. Pearce, 91 P.3d 605, 624 (Okla. 2004).

76. State ex rel. State Bd. of Embalmers & Funeral Directors v. Stone Casket Co. of Oklahoma City, 976 P.2d 1074, 1076 (1998).

77. This term owes its origin to the work of historian Eric Foner, who contended in his book FREE SOIL, FREE LABOR, FREE MEN (1971) that the "free labor ideology" of economic independence was an advent of the nineteenth century. This is misleading, however, because anti-slavery thinking was in fact a fairly obvious application of the classical liberalism articulated in the Declaration of Independence and the Constitution, antedating the abolitionist movement by well over a century.

78. In his infamous decision in *State v. Mann*, 13 N.C. 263, 266 (1829), Chief Justice Thomas Ruffin defined slavery as the condition of being "doomed in [one's] own person . . . to toil that another may reap the fruits."

someone of the rewards of his or her industry is to deprive that person of part of the self—to compel that person's labor.[79]

Eighteenth- and nineteenth-century Americans would have viewed this moral problem in terms of biblical morality, and the phrase "fruits of one's labor" originates in biblical discourse. It refers to the farmer who, on account of Adam's curse,[80] must toil for his food—and whose labors produce literal fruits, to which he has a moral claim. Conversely, it refers to the vision of political justice repeatedly referred to in the Bible as the freedom of each person to "sit every man under his vine and under his fig tree, [where] none shall make them afraid."[81] Christian abolitionists regarded slavery as sinful because, as one of them put it, slavery "deprives the slave of himself in the outset, and then deprives him of all the fruits of his labor," given that "the slave does not receive for his labor the same compensation that a freeman does. . . . That leading element of slavery is to exact from the slave *more* that he receives. . . . The Bible, therefore, which demands that the laborer shall receive just compensation, condemns slavery, in condemning the withholding of just and equal wages."[82] The opposite of slavery, for which abolitionists and their allies struggled, was a system in which each individual was free to support himself or herself through work, without the unjustified interference of others—including the state. "What is freedom?" demanded the escaped slave Frederick Douglass, and he answered, "It is the right to choose one's own employment . . . and when any individual or combination of individuals undertakes to decide for any man when he shall work, where he shall work, at what he shall work, and for what he shall work, he or they practically reduce him to slavery."[83] Every person, said Abraham Lincoln, has "the right to eat the bread, without leave of anybody else, which his own hand earns,"[84] and this right

---

79. *See* ROBERT NOZICK, ANARCHY, STATE, AND UTOPIA 290–91 (1974).

80. Genesis 3:19.

81. Micah 4:4. *Cf.* 1 Kings 4:25; Zechariah 3:10. This was George Washington's favorite biblical metaphor for politics. *See* Daniel L. Dreisbach, *The 'Vine and Fig Tree' in George Washington's Letters: Reflections on a Biblical Motif in the Literature of the American Founding Era*, 76 ANGLICAN & EPISCOPAL HISTORY 299 (2007).

82. 1 CHARLES ELLIOTT, SINFULNESS OF AMERICAN SLAVERY PROVED FROM ITS EVIL SOURCES 262 (1850).

83. Frederick Douglass, *What the Black Man Wants* (1865), *in* GREAT SPEECHES BY FREDERICK DOUGLASS 52 (James Daley ed., 2013).

84. First Debate with Stephen Douglas, Aug. 21, 1858, *in* 3 COLLECTED WORKS OF ABRAHAM LINCOLN 16 (R. Basler ed., 1953).

is the foundation of the "just and generous, and prosperous system" of economic liberty "which opens the way for all—gives hope to all, and energy, and progress, and improvement of condition to all."[85]

Any law which, without adequate justification, deprives a person of the right to labor for oneself plainly contradicts this principle,[86] which was written into the Missouri Constitution while Lincoln was still living.[87] To view the "fruits of one's labor" clause as concerned only with slavery is thus "far-fetched,"[88] especially given that the clause has been reincorporated in every subsequent iteration of the Missouri Constitution and those that followed, notwithstanding the abolition of slavery. A better reading of the clause is that it was intended to preserve economic liberty against unwarranted interference, and to do so more specifically and with greater legal strength than the federal constitution provides.

B. Anti-Monopoly and Anti–Special Privilege Clauses

As an historical matter, legal protections for economic liberty in the United States trace their origin to the campaign of seventeenth-century English Whigs against the arbitrary monopolies established by the Stuart monarchs.[89] These monopolies consisted of exclusive trading rights that allowed only a single practitioner to operate in a specified business—for example, prohibiting anyone but the patent holder from selling playing cards in London.[90] By the time of the American Revolution, it was well established (at least among Whigs) that such monopolies violated the Magna Carta's "law of the land" clause because they deprived people of the opportunity to earn a living for themselves

---

85. Speech at Wisconsin Fair, Sept. 30, 1859, in *id.* at 479.

86. *Cf.* Yick Wo v. Hopkins, 118 U.S. 356, 370 (1886) (striking down a standardless permit requirement for business because "the very idea that one man may be compelled to hold his life, or the means of living, or any material right essential to the enjoyment of life, at the mere will of another, seems to be intolerable in any country where freedom prevails, as being the essence of slavery itself.").

87. The "fruits of one's labor" clause was introduced in the Missouri Constitutional Convention on February 25, 1865. *See* JOURNAL OF THE MISSOURI STATE CONVENTION 117 (1865).

88. Kansas City Premier Apartments, Inc. v. Missouri Real Est. Comm'n, 344 S.W.3d 160, 174 n.6 (Mo. 2011) (Wolff, J., dissenting).

89. *See generally* Steven G. Calabresi & Larissa C. Leibowitz, *Monopolies and the Constitution: A History of Crony Capitalism*, 36 HARV. J.L. & PUB. POL'Y 983 (2013); TIMOTHY SANDEFUR, THE RIGHT TO EARN A LIVING: ECONOMIC FREEDOM AND THE LAW ch. 2 (2010).

90. The Case of Monopolies, 77 Eng. Rep. 1260 (Q.B. 1603).

in a common occupation. Indeed, the Massachusetts Body of Liberties of 1641 declared that "no monopolies shall be granted or allowed amongst us," with the exception of patents for inventions, and even then, only "for a short time."[91]

State constitutions began including anti-monopoly clauses and clauses prohibiting special privileges or special laws in the nineteenth century.[92] Prohibitions on monopolies and special privileges were written out of a concern to prohibit the government from descending into cronyism and factionalism. Unfortunately, thanks to the influence of modern "judicial restraint" ideology, many state courts today apply something akin to rational basis review when considering lawsuits that raise arguments under these clauses. As is well known, rational basis deference effectively neutralizes the ability of courts to counteract such cronyism, notwithstanding their constitutional obligation to do so.[93] Thus, for example, the Connecticut Supreme Court has said, in applying its anti–special privileges clause, that a law is not a special privilege if it advances a public purpose, and that it is the legislature's role to determine what constitutes a public purpose; courts may intercede only if the legislature's action is "manifestly and palpably incorrect."[94] Other courts employ similarly deferential standards.[95] This effectively legalizes the privileges that these constitutions expressly forbid.[96]

Arizona's prohibition on special laws offers an exception. The Arizona Constitution prohibits "local or special laws," with certain specified exceptions.[97] And the state's courts have fashioned an effective test for when a law constitutes a special law. First, they have held that the clause is not merely an equality requirement: a law can be an

---

91. Mass. Body of Liberties § 9 (1641). *Cf.* U.S. CONST. art. I, § 8, cl. 8 (allowing intellectual property only for "limited times").

92. Connecticut's, adopted in 1818, seems to have been the first. Calabresi & Leibowitz, *supra* note 89 at 1077.

93. *See* Hettinga v. United States, 677 F.3d 471, 482–83 (D.C. Cir. 2012) (Brown, J., concurring).

94. Kinney v. State, 941 A.2d 907, 914 (Conn. 2008) (quoting Chotkowski v. State, 690 A.2d 368 (1997)).

95. *See, e.g.*, White v. State, 88 Cal. App. 4th 298, 311 (2001) (applying extreme deference to state constitution's anti–special privileges clause).

96. To borrow Justice Greene Bronson's oft-quoted phrase, the rational basis test changes constitutional prohibitions into an instruction that tells legislators, "You shall not do the wrong, unless you choose to do it." Taylor v. Porter, 4 Hill 140, 145 (N.Y. Sup. Ct. 1843).

97. ARIZ. CONST. art. IV, pt. 2, § 19.

unconstitutional special law even if it does not violate the equal protection mandate.[98] Second, a law is a special law if it lacks a rational connection to a legitimate government purpose.[99] Third, the court must determine of the class of persons to which the law applies is "open" or "closed," meaning that the law must apply to a group that is identified in such a way that it is possible for future persons to come within its scope, and possible for those to whom the law currently applies to leave its ambit.[100] This means a law that applies only to, say, "the restaurant currently located on First and Main Streets" is unconstitutional, because it is not possible for another restaurant to become that restaurant, and it is not possible for that restaurant to cease to be what it is—whereas a law that applies to "any restaurant that shall be located at First and Main Streets" would pass constitutional muster, since it's possible for the restaurant that currently exists there to go out of business, and possible to start a new one. This is a lenient but still meaningful test that gives legislators the flexibility necessary to shape the law to suit a variety of exigencies, but still limits their ability to engage in cronyism. Other states should adopt a similar approach.[101]

Anti-monopoly clauses, too, have proven effective in some states. True, some states have adopted a rational basis–type standard that essentially neuters the clause. Tennessee courts, for example, have said that "the anti-monopoly clause of our constitution does not prohibit the legislature from granting a monopoly . . . [if it] has a reasonable tendency to aid in the promotion of the health, safety, morals and well being of the people."[102] This is illogical, because the legislature can be expected to assert that whatever it does, no matter how wrongful, has a reasonable tendency to promote the public good. Moreover, the anti-monopoly clause was adopted specifically to limit the *means* by which the legislature may promote the public good. A law that abridges a person's liberty

98. Arizona Downs v. Arizona Horsemen's Foundation, 637 P.2d 1053, 1060 (Ariz. 1981).

99. Petitioners for Deannexation v. City of Goodyear, 773 P.2d 1026, 1031 (Ariz. Ct. App. 1989).

100. Republic Inv. Fund I v. Town of Surprise, 800 P.2d 1251, 1257 (Ariz. 1990).

101. Nebraska, Florida, and Wisconsin employ a similar "closed class" test. Haman v. Marsh, 467 N.W.2d 836, 845 (Neb. 1991); City of Miami v. McGrath, 824 So. 2d 143, 154 (Fla. 2002); Madison Metro. Sewerage Dist. v. Stein, 177 N.W.2d 131, 137–38 (Wis. 1970). Texas does, too, but it still allows closed classes if they pass rational basis review, which, again, essentially neuters the protection. Pub. Util. Comm'n of Texas v. Sw. Water Servs., Inc., 636 S.W.2d 262, 266 (Tex. App. 1982). In *Fla. Dep't of Health v. Florigrown, LLC*, 317 So. 3d 1101, 1120 (Fla. 2021) (Lawson, J., concurring), Justice Lawson warned against this problem.

102. *See, e.g.*, Checker Cab Co. v. City of Johnson City, 216 S.W.2d 335, 337 (Tenn. 1948).

without reasonably tending to promote the public good already violates various *other* constitutional prohibitions, such as the law of the land clause,[103] and there is no reason to believe the anti-monopoly clause was intended as a mere redundancy of that basic requirement. Rather, the latter clause was adopted out of a belief that the ordinary political process and the basic requirement that government use its powers for the public welfare were insufficient to protect against the evils of cronyism. In short, it prohibits the legislature from promoting the public good *via monopolies.*

In other states, however, the prohibition on monopolies has proven a meaningful protection against government restrictions on economic liberty. In 2016, for example, when a Little Rock entrepreneur brought a lawsuit challenging that city's monopoly on the taxicab industry, the trial court relied on that state's anti-monopoly clause to reject the city's motion to dismiss.[104] (The case settled in the plaintiff's favor.) In 1979, the Georgia Supreme Court declared that provisions of the state's Franchise Practices Act—which restricted the number of automobile dealerships that could operate within a geographical area, to prevent economic competition—violated the state's anti-monopoly clause.[105]

One major challenge in this area is the judge-made doctrine of state immunity. Although anti-monopoly clauses appear to never include any exemption for the government, state courts have often manufactured such exemptions.[106] This is no different from the judge-made doctrine of *Parker* immunity.[107] In such cases, judges simply declare by fiat that a constitutional provision that absolutely prohibits, without reservation, all monopolies, nonetheless somehow permits them—and they do so, moreover, in precisely those circumstances that the authors of these clauses had in mind: government-enforced exclusive trading rights. There is nothing to be said against the illogic of this notion except that there is nothing to be said for it: state anti-monopoly clauses were written to

---

103. *See, e.g.,* Campbell v. McIntyre, 52 S.W.2d 162, 164 (Tenn. 1932); Wright v. Wiles, 117 S.W.2d 736, 738–39 (Tenn. 1938); Livesay v. Tenn. Bd. of Exam'rs in Watchmaking, 322 S.W.2d 209, 213 (Tenn. 1959).

104. Ken's Cab, LLC, & Ken Leininger v. City of Little Rock, No. 60CV-16-1260 (Pulaski Co. Cir. Ct. 2016).

105. Georgia Franchise Pracs. Comm'n v. Massey-Ferguson, Inc., 262 S.E.2d 106 (Ga. 1979). The state later amended its constitution to create an exception to the anti-monopoly clause that permits monopolies in the case of automobile dealerships. GA. CONST. art. III, § 6, ¶ 5(c)(2).

106. *See, e.g.,* Charles Uhden, Inc. v. Greenough, 43 P.2d 983, 987 (1935).

107. Parker v. Brown, 317 U.S. 341 (1943).

forbid the government from outlawing free competition. To exempt the state from such provisions is manifestly illogical and unjust.

C. Pursuit of Happiness Clauses

Several state constitutions include a guarantee of the right to "pursue happiness."[108] This right, of course, must include the right to economic liberty, which is one of the chief means of pursuing happiness. Indeed, the phrase—which obviously traces its lineage to the Declaration of Independence[109]—was fashioned by Thomas Jefferson as a simplification of George Mason's phrasing in the Virginia Declaration of Rights: "[A]ll men are by nature equally free and independent and have certain inherent rights, of which, when they enter into a state of society, they cannot, by any compact, deprive or divest their posterity; namely, the enjoyment of life and liberty, with the means of acquiring and possessing property, and pursuing and obtaining happiness and safety."[110] The capacity to enjoy liberty with the means of acquiring property to obtain happiness obviously encompasses the right to provide for oneself through the use of one's faculties, including the freedom to make employment contracts, or to make and sell items or provide services for pay. It was certainly understood in this way at the time of the framing.

State courts have held that the "pursuit of happiness" clauses in state constitutions protect the right to pursue a lawful occupation. In *Myers v. City of Defiance*,[111] for example, the Ohio Court of Appeals held that a city ordinance requiring licenses for dry cleaners violated the pursuit of happiness clause, where it imposed a financial burden on out-of-city businesses. The court declared that the pursuit of happiness clause was "the legal equivalent" of the due process clause of the Fourteenth Amendment,[112] but did not

---

108. *See, e.g.*, OHIO CONST. art. I, § 1; IND. CONST. art. I, § 1. Thanks to U.S. influences, even the constitutions of Japan and Korea include such clauses. REPUB. KOREA CONST. ch. 2, art. X; JAPAN CONST. art. XIII. *See further* Jibong Kim, *Pursuit of Happiness Clause in the Korean Constitution*, 1 J. KOREAN L. 71 (2001). In *City of Sioux City v. Jacobsma*, 862 N.W.2d 335, 348–53 (Iowa 2015), the Iowa Supreme Court offered an enlightening discussion of that state's pursuit of happiness clause, and compared it to those of other states.

109. 1 Stat. 1 (1776). *See further* Carli N. Conklin, *The Origins of the Pursuit of Happiness*, 7 WASH. U. JURISPRUDENCE REV. 195 (2015).

110. Va. Decl. of Rights ¶ 1 (1776).

111. *See, e.g.*, Myers v. City of Defiance, 36 N.E.2d 162, 166–67 (Ohio Ct. App. 1940).

112. *Id.* at 168.

apply rational basis review; instead, it found that by discriminating against business owners from out of town, the ordinance "constitutes an attempt to distinguish between persons engaged in the same business merely on the basis of the location of their business houses," which was unconstitutional.[113] In *Kirtley v. State*,[114] the Indiana Supreme Court[115] declared a state law prohibiting "scalping" unconstitutional under its pursuit of happiness clause. The clause protects "the right of every one to be free in the use of their powers in the pursuit of happiness in such calling as they may choose subject only to the restraints necessary to secure the common welfare," said the court, and a law that "prohibits that which is harmless in itself, or requires that to be done which does not tend to promote the health, comfort, morality, safety or welfare of society," exceeds the state's regulatory power.[116]

D. Confronting the Dogma of Deference

Of course, identifying the source of constitutional protection for individual liberty is only part of the process. The greater challenge is whether courts will exercise meaningful judgment in enforcing the clause in question, or whether they will succumb to what I call the dogma of deference—"rational basis" and its allied notions.[117] The dogma is better viewed as a sophisticated kind of folk philosophy than a jurisprudential theory, in part because it is often premised on the rejection of theory *per se*.[118] The idea of judicial deference to the will of the majority cannot be substantiated on a rigorous enough basis to deserve the name "theory,"[119] and cannot account for so simple a right as the right to

---

113. *Id.* at 169.

114. 84 N.E.2d 712 (Ind. 1949).

115. An extensive discussion of the history of the Indiana clause appears in *Members of Med. Licensing Bd. of Indiana v. Planned Parenthood Great Nw., Hawai'i, Alaska, Indiana, Kentucky, Inc.*, 211 N.E.3d 957, 967–75 (Ind. 2023).

116. *Id.* at 714.

117. *See* Timothy Sandefur, *The Dogma of Deference*, 18 TEX. REV. L. & POL. 121 (2013).

118. *See, e.g.*, J. HARVIE WILKINSON, COSMIC CONSTITUTIONAL THEORY (2012); *see further* Timothy Sandefur, *Hercules and Narragansett among the Originalists*, 39 REASON PAPERS 8, 8–13 (2017) (discussing Wilkinson's cynicism).

119. The best effort to do so is the notion of "democracy reinforcement" championed by John Hart Ely, in DEMOCRACY AND DISTRUST (1980). This theory, however, gets the entire constitutional scheme backward. *See generally* Roger Pilon, *A Court without a Compass*, 40 N.Y.L. SCH. L. REV. 999 (1996).

refuse to participate in democratic politics, such as was at issue in *West Virginia Board of Education v. Barnette.*[120]

Be that as it may, state courts are often tempted to adopt something along the lines of rational basis review with respect to state constitutional guarantees of economic liberty. They have done so with respect to clauses forbidding monopolies,[121] privileges,[122] subsidies,[123] and special laws,[124] as well as pursuit of happiness clauses,[125] fruits of one's labor clauses,[126] and protections against eminent domain.[127]

As a doctrinal matter, this makes little sense. The rational basis test was invented in 1934 by the federal Supreme Court in *Nebbia v. New York.*[128] It was intended for use when applying the Due Process Clause of the Fourteenth Amendment, and was created in response to criticisms of so-called substantive due process during the "*Lochner* era." Those criticisms consisted—and still consist—partly of the idea that "due process," correctly interpreted, only guarantees "procedural" fairness, and does not wall off a category of rights from legislative interference, as courts were accused of doing in the years before the Depression.[129] Rather, (the theory goes), the legislative process simply *is* "due process," at least with respect to economic liberty and private property rights.[130] A second, parallel,

---

120. 319 U.S. 624 (1943).

121. *See, e.g., Checker Cab Co.*, 216 S.W.2d at 337.

122. *See, e.g.,* De La Fuente v. Simon, 940 N.W.2d 477, 488 (Minn. 2020).

123. *See, e.g.,* Tosto v. Pennsylvania Nursing Home Loan Agency, 331 A.2d 198, 202 (Pa. 1975).

124. *See, e.g.,* City of Aurora v. Spectra Commc'ns Grp., LLC, 592 S.W.3d 764 (Mo. 2019).

125. *See, e.g.,* Garrison v. New Fashion Pork LLP, 977 N.W.2d 67, 83–84 (Iowa 2022).

126. *See, e.g., Fisher*, 948 S.W.2d at 610.

127. *See, e.g.,* Portland Co. v. City of Portland, 979 A.2d 1279, 1288 (Me. 2009).

128. 291 U.S. 502 (1934). Of course, the Court modeled it on theories that had been circulating in the preceding decades. *See, e.g.,* James Thayer, *The Origin and Scope of the American Doctrine of Constitutional Law*, 7 HARV. L. REV. 129 (1893). *See further* G. Edward White, *Revisiting Substantive Due Process and Holmes's Lochner Dissent*, 63 BROOK. L. REV. 87, 108–10 (1997) (discussing early twentieth-century criticisms of substantive due process).

129. For a full discussion of why the criticisms of substantive due process were and are misguided, see TIMOTHY SANDEFUR, THE CONSCIENCE OF THE CONSTITUTION chs. 3 & 4 (2013).

130. This is often phrased as "[w]here the legislature enacts general legislation . . . adjusting the benefits and burdens of economic life . . . 'the legislative determination provides all the process that is due.'" Hoffman v. City of Warwick, 909 F.2d 608, 619–20 (1st Cir. 1990). *See also* Obergefell v. Hodges, 576 U.S. 644, 705 (2015) (Scalia, J., dissenting) ("There is indeed a process due the people on issues of this sort—the democratic process.").

criticism of substantive due process that led to the creation of rational basis scrutiny was rooted in federalism: it was wrong, critics charged, for federal courts to bar states from "experimenting" with economic regulations by a strict application of substantive due process.[131]

In short, rational basis review was supposed to eliminate substantive restrictions from a constitutional provision that was concerned solely with process, and to instead serve the goal of "representation reinforcement"—ensuring that the legislative process was conducted in a proper manner.

Once we appreciate these rationales, it should be obvious why importing rational basis into clauses other than the Due Process Clause is fallacious. Obviously, the federalism concerns that gave rise to rational basis review cannot apply to state courts, since their rulings *are* federalism. But neither can the "representation-reinforcement" rationale—that due process only requires courts to ensure that the legislative procedures operate fairly—justify adapting rational basis into constitutional provisions that are not concerned with process. That is, even assuming that the Due Process Clause only provides procedural, not substantive protections, it makes no sense to use rational basis when applying anti-monopoly clauses, gift clauses, pursuit of happiness clauses, and other constitutional provisions that certainly *do* prohibit substantive outcomes. These clauses aren't even superficially concerned with *procedure*, so the "process"-oriented concern about "judicial activism" cannot logically apply here.

Remarkably, *Nebbia* itself seems to have anticipated this problem. In the sentence announcing the rational basis test, it said, "[S]o far as the requirement of due process is concerned, *and in the absence of other constitutional restriction*, a state is free to adopt whatever economic policy may reasonably be deemed to promote public welfare."[132] And the Court reiterated this point in *Carolene Products*: "There may be narrower scope for operation of the presumption of constitutionality when legislation appears on its face to be within a specific prohibition of the Constitution."[133]

In short, applying rational basis review outside the context of due process is a category error. It also has the consequence of rendering other clauses duplicative of the due

---

131. *See, e.g.*, New State Ice Co. v. Liebmann, 285 U.S. 262, 280 (1932) (Brandeis, J., dissenting).

132. 291 U.S. at 537 (emphasis added).

133. United States v. Carolene Prod. Co., 304 U.S. 144, 153 n.4 (1938).

process clause. To read, say, a constitutional prohibition on special legislation as requiring nothing more than what the Due Process Clause already requires—that is, that a law reasonably advance a conceivable public good—commits a serious interpretive sin: it makes distinct constitutional provisions into redundant surplusage.[134] Constitutional prohibitions on special laws, monopolies, subsidies, and so forth were added to state constitutions out of a belief that the legislative process, and the minimum requirement of rationality, were *insufficient* to ensure against these specific *substantive* abuses. A rational basis approach—which is premised on the idea that the legislative process is sufficient to protect constitutional values—is therefore inappropriate.

The rationality requirement applies across the board to everything government does. But certain types of injustices—including monopolies, subsidies, special privileges, restrictions on the pursuit of happiness—are not necessarily *irrational* or *arbitrary* in the sense contemplated by the Due Process Clause, because there's virtually always *some* colorable argument in favor of them. That's why the authors of state constitutions were not satisfied to adopt just the Due Process Clause, but also added the additional prohibitions—to prohibit these outcomes *even where* they may not be so egregious as to be classified as irrational. Subsidies, for example, are virtually always indulged in because lawmakers think they will ultimately redound to society's benefit; indeed, the dictionary actually defines "subsidy" as a payment to a private entity motivated by the government's belief that the recipient is "likely to be of benefit to the public."[135] So for a court to hold that financial aid to a private recipient is not an unconstitutional subsidy if legislators thought the recipient would benefit the public is, again, fallacious.

Another reason it makes no sense to incorporate *Nebbia*'s rational basis theory into a state's due process jurisprudence is that most state due process clauses were written before 1934, and their authors cannot have believed that readers of those clauses would understand them as incorporating the rational basis test. As Justice Parker observed in *State v. Lupo,*[136] the Alabama Constitution was written in 1901.[137] Those who wrote and

---

134. *Cf.* Jack L. Landau, *An Introduction to Oregon Constitutional Interpretation,* 55 WILLAMETTE L. REV. 261, 281–84 (2019) (examining presumption against redundancy).

135. *See* BLACK'S LAW DICTIONARY 1117 (1910) ("subsidy").

136. 984 So. 2d 395, 407 (Ala. 2007) (Parker, J., concurring).

137. Alabama adopted a new constitution in 2022, but it consisted only of a recodification of the existing constitution, with racist language removed and certain sections reorganized.

ratified that state's due process clause were presumably aware of the prevalent understanding of "due process of law," which in 1901 included meaningful protections for economic liberty. To implement instead the rational-basis theory fashioned by federal courts in 1934 is therefore anachronistic.[138]

As for the flaws of the rational basis test itself, these are now well known and well documented. Legal scholars have explained that the test—at least as applied today—is so deferential as to result in irrational and indefensible outcomes.[139] Many judges have gone on record about the problems with a deference so extreme that it blinds courts to constitutional violations. These include Justice Willett's concurrence in *Patel v. Texas Department of Licensing & Regulation*,[140] Judge Brown's concurrence in *Hettinga v. United States*,[141] Justice Stegall's dissent in *Hodes & Nauser*,[142] Justice Bolick's concurrence in *State v. Arevalo*,[143] and Justice Bradley's dissent in *Porter v. State*.[144] Critiques like these have led several state courts either to reject rational basis review or to adopt a version of it that focuses on actual facts—that is, a version that does not hypothesize potential rationalizations for a challenged law, as the federal rational basis test appears to.[145] These courts

138. *Lupo*, 984 So. 2d at 408–09 (Parker, J., concurring).

139. *See, e.g.*, James M. McGoldrick, Jr., *The Rational Basis Test and Why It Is So Irrational: An Eighty-Year Retrospective*, 55 SAN DIEGO L. REV. 751 (2018); Steve Sanders, *Making It Up: Lessons for Equal Protection Doctrine from the Use and Abuse of Hypothesized Purposes in the Marriage Equality Litigation*, 68 HASTINGS L.J. 657 (2017); Tara A. Smith, *A Conceivable Constitution: How the Rational Basis Test Throws Darts and Misses the Mark*, 59 S. TEX. L. REV. 77 (2017). Clark Neily, *No Such Thing: Litigating Under the Rational Basis Test*, 1 N.Y.U. J.L. & LIBERTY 898 (2005).

140. 469 S.W.3d 69, 92 (Tex. 2015) (Willett, J., concurring).

141. 677 F.3d 471, 480 (D.C. Cir. 2012) (Brown, J., concurring).

142. 440 P.3d at 550–51 (Stegall, J., dissenting).

143. 470 P.3d 644, 652 (2020) (Bolick, J., concurring).

144. 913 N.W.2d 842, 852 (Wis. 2018) (Bradley, J., concurring).

145. In *F.C.C. v. Beach Commc'ns, Inc.*, 508 U.S. 307, 315 (1993), the U.S. Supreme Court said that under the federal rational basis test, it is "entirely irrelevant for constitutional purposes whether the conceived reason for the challenged distinction actually motivated the legislature," meaning that courts can uphold the constitutionality of legislation "based on [a judge's] rational speculation unsupported by evidence or empirical data." But it later indicated that rational basis review does *not* entitle a court to simply manufacture justification for a challenged law. *See, e.g.*, Heller v. Doe, 509 U.S. 312, 321 (1993) ("even the standard of rationality as we so often have defined it must find some footing in the realities of the subject addressed by the legislation."). In fact, the Supreme Court has wavered between these two positions for decades. *See* Timothy Sandefur, *Rational Basis and the 12(b)(6) Motion: An Unnecessary "Perplexity,"* 25 GEO. MASON U. CIV. RTS. L.J. 43, 59–63 (2014). Remarkably, only nine months after it unveiled the rational basis test, the Supreme Court said in *Borden's Farm Prod. Co. v. Baldwin*, 293 U.S. 194, 209 (1934), that the presumption of constitutionality, "is a rebuttable presumption . . . not a conclusive presumption, or a

include the Georgia,[146] Pennsylvania,[147] Iowa,[148] Vermont,[149] Alaska,[150] Utah,[151] and New Mexico[152] Supreme Courts.[153]

These courts have recognized that rationality review as currently practiced tends to blind courts to the kinds of factionalism and "naked preferences"[154] that the Constitution was written to prevent. Absent meaningful judicial checks and balances, the legislative process tends to be "captured" by special interests who stand to gain financially from prohibiting economic competition from entrepreneurs and newcomers in the market.[155] Constitutional limits on the legislature were created specifically to counteract this tendency, meaning that lax rationality review tends to remove one of the legs of the constitutional stool. Deference can therefore be characterized as a form of "judicial activism" in itself.[156] The practitioner seeking to defend economic liberty before state courts should be prepared to explain why a blindfold-style rational basis test[157] is inappropriate as a matter of law and history, and why it fosters the kinds of injustices that constitutional provisions were intended to prevent.

---

rule of law which makes legislative action invulnerable to constitutional assault." It repeated this point in *Nashville, C. & S. L. Railway v. Walters, Nashville C. & S. L. Ry. v. Walters*, 294 U.S. 405, 414–15 (1935). *Polk Co. v. Glover*, 305 U.S. 5, 9–10 (1938), and *Carolene Products*, 304 U.S. at 153–54.

146. *Raffenperger*, 888 S.E.2d at 492.

147. *Ladd*, 230 A.3d at 1108.

148. City of Sioux City v. Jacobsma, 862 N.W.2d 335, 347–48 (Iowa 2015).

149. Baker v. State, 744 A.2d 864, 871–73 (Vt. 1999).

150. Isakson v. Rickey, 550 P.2d 359, 362 (Alaska. 1976).

151. Mountain Fuel Supply Co. v. Salt Lake City Corp., 752 P.2d 884, 889 (Utah 1988).

152. Rodriguez v. Brand W. Dairy, 378 P.3d 13, 25–26 (N.M. 2016).

153. *See further* James C. Kirby, Jr., *Expansive Judicial Review of Economic Regulation under State Constitutions: The Case for Realism*, 48 TENN. L. REV. 241 (1981).

154. Cass R. Sunstein, *Naked Preferences and the Constitution*, 84 COLUM. L. REV. 1689 (1984).

155. *See generally* Paul J. Larkin, Jr., *Public Choice Theory and Occupational Licensing*, 39 HARV. J.L. & PUB. POL'Y 209 (2016); Donald J. Kochan, *"Public Use" and the Independent Judiciary: Condemnation in an Interest-Group Perspective*, 3 TEX. REV. L. & POL. 49 (1998).

156. *See, e.g.*, United States v. Carlton, 512 U.S. 26, 41 (1994) (Scalia, J., concurring) ("The picking and choosing among various rights to be accorded 'substantive due process' protection is alone enough to arouse suspicion; but the categorical and inexplicable exclusion of so-called 'economic rights' . . . unquestionably involves policymaking rather than neutral legal analysis.").

157. *See* Arceneaux v. Treen, 671 F.2d 128, 136 n.3 (5th Cir. 1982) (Goldberg, J., concurring) (rationality review "invites us to cup our hands over our eyes and then imagine if there could be anything right with the statute.").

What's more, to the degree that rational basis review results in judicial rubber-stamping of legislative or executive action, it conflicts with the separation of powers clauses that appear in many state constitutions. These are usually phrased in quite strict language. New Jersey's, for example, says, "The powers of the government shall be divided among three distinct branches, the legislative, executive, and judicial. No person or persons belonging to or constituting one branch shall exercise any of the powers properly belonging to either of the others, except as expressly provided in this Constitution."[158] The federal constitution, of course, contains no express separation of powers clause. These provisions were therefore written with a particular eye to reinforcing the checks and balances system and making it stronger than in the federal sphere.[159]

The Supreme Court recently overruled the doctrine of judicial deference to administrative interpretations of law (known as *Chevron* deference) on the grounds that such deference is inconsistent with the Administrative Procedure Act.[160] Some states refused to adopt such a doctrine to begin with, for separation of powers reasons.[161] But separation of powers principles must militate even more strongly against a standard of *legislative* deference such as rational basis review, which allows the legislators to impose whatever burdens on individual rights they consider reasonable. If "[t]he separation of powers prevents [state courts] from abdicating core power," as the Wisconsin Supreme Court has said,[162] then courts should refuse to uphold economic burdens simply on the basis that lawmakers considered them a good idea.

In *Nollan v. California Coastal Commission*[163] and *District of Columbia v. Heller*,[164] the U.S. Supreme Court offered some insight on when a rational basis test should or should not apply to a constitutional right. *Nollan* concerned the kinds of demands a state may make on a property owner in exchange for a development permit. Justice Brennan, in dissent,

---

158. N.J. CONST. art. III, § 1. Some states, on the other hand, have more general separation of powers clauses. *See* Jim Rossi, *Institutional Design and the Lingering Legacy of Antifederalist Separation of Powers Ideals in the States*, 52 VAND. L. REV. 1167, 1190–91 (1999).

159. *See generally* Tarr, *supra* note 21.

160. Loper Bright Enters. v. Raimondo, 144 S. Ct. 2244, 2248 (2024).

161. *See, e.g., In re* Complaint of Rovas Against SBC Michigan, 754 N.W.2d 259, 262 (Mich. 2008).

162. *Tetra Tech EC*, 914 N.W.2d at 42.

163. 483 U.S. 825 (1987).

164. 554 U.S. 570 (2008).

argued that the condition merely needs to have a rational connection to the purposes of the permit, but the majority rejected this because there was "no reason to believe" that "the standards for takings challenges, due process challenges, and equal protection challenges are identical."[165] Again, in *Heller*, the Court was confronted with a rare question: What standard of review should apply to a constitutional right that the Court had never before recognized? Again, the dissent recommended a rational basis standard, but again the majority said no: such a low standard applied only to "constitutional commands that are themselves prohibitions on irrational laws,"[166] such as prohibitions on arbitrary discrimination by the state, and was *not* appropriate when a court must "evaluate the extent to which a legislature may regulate a specific, enumerated right."[167] To apply rational basis in such a case would make the latter protection "redundant [of] the separate constitutional prohibitions on irrational laws," such as the Due Process Clause.[168]

These cases offer helpful arguments against the adoption of rational basis—and they also suggest that the burden of persuasion is not on plaintiffs who ask the courts to apply a meaningful degree of judicial review, but is instead properly placed on those government defendants who advocate a rational basis standard, because adopting such a standard would be taking a step down from the ordinary baseline of judicial skepticism. Such a reduction of standards requires a good justification.

E. Trade Triggers

One form of irrationality to which courts have so far paid insufficient attention lies in the government regulating certain activities when they are engaged in for money, but not when they are engaged in for free. For example, in some states, a person may cut another person's hair for free without a license, but anyone who cuts hair for money must get a barber license.[169] One recent Kansas case involved a city ordinance that allowed people to keep bees in their backyards without a license, so long as they gave away the honey. But if the same person kept the same bees in the same yard and *sold* the honey,

---

165. 483 U.S. at 834 n.3.
166. *Id.* at 628 n.27.
167. *Id.*
168. *Id.*
169. *See, e.g.,* TEX. OCC. CODE § 1603.0011(a) (requiring a license if one treats hair "for compensation").

she was engaging in a "home-based business" involving animals—a crime punishable by six months in jail and a $500 fine for *each day* of the offense.[170]

This is patently irrational. I call these "trade trigger" laws,[171] analogous to the "speech trigger" found unconstitutional in *Holder v. Humanitarian Law Project*.[172] In that case, the Court declared a law unconstitutional because "the conduct triggering coverage under the statute consists of communicating a message."[173] In a "trade trigger" situation, the conduct triggering coverage under the statute consists solely of the exchange of money.

But in the ordinary case, it's arbitrary and irrational for the state to draw a line based solely on the exchange of funds. If it's safe for a person to cut hair without money, nothing about the exchange of money makes that haircut less safe. Nothing about the exchange of money changes the nature of the activity or provides adequate reason for requiring a person to obtain the state's permission to engage in that activity.[174] There may be exceptions; some activities inherently involve the exchange of money (brokerage, for example[175]), and obviously the exchange of money raises the possibility of fraud or false advertising. But laws against fraud or false advertising already address that concern. Thus it is presumptively irrational for the state to allow, say, people to engage in "lactation consulting" without a license so long as they do it on a *volunteer* basis, but to require extensive educational, training, and testing requirements if they do precisely the same thing for compensation.[176] If a law fails the rational basis test when it "undercuts the principle of non-contradiction,"[177] then it is positively irrational to impose a license on

170. *See* Finnerty v. City of Ottawa (Franklin Co. Dist. Ct. FR-2023-CV-000046, filed May 22, 2023).

171. Sandefur, *Rebuilding*, *supra* note 1 at 285–96.

172. 561 U.S. 1 (2010).

173. *Id.* at 28.

174. *Cf.* JASON F. BRENNAN & PETER JAWORSKI, MARKETS WITHOUT LIMITS: MORAL VIRTUES AND COMMERCIAL INTERESTS 10 (2016) ("[T]he market does not transform what were permissible acts into impermissible acts" or vice versa).

175. Under federal law, the exchange of money is *not* the trigger for the application of broker licensing requirements. *See, e.g.*, United States Sec. & Exch. Comm'n v. Collyard, 861 F.3d 760, 766–67 (8th Cir. 2017) (describing multifactor test for determining when someone is a broker).

176. *See* Brief Amicus Curiae of Goldwater Institute and Pacific Legal Foundation in Support of Appellants, Jackson v. Raffensperger (Ga. No. S20A0039), https://www.goldwaterinstitute.org/wp-content/uploads/2022/04/Goldwater-PLFs-Amicus-Curiae-Brief-in-Support-of-Jackson190913.pdf.

177. Merrifield v. Lockyer, 547 F.3d 978, 991 (9th Cir. 2008).

an activity when engaged in for money, but not when done for free. The creation of arbitrary exemptions from a licensing requirement has often been viewed as evidence that the requirement itself is irrational.[178] Where the state imposes a regulatory burden on an activity triggered solely by the exchange of money, that fact should be at least presumptive evidence that the burden is irrational.

F. Permit Freedom

In a series of cases starting in the 1950s, the U.S. Supreme Court declared that whenever the government imposes a permit requirement on an activity, certain "procedural safe-guards" must be in place: the criteria for obtaining the permit must be clear and unambiguous; the applicant must be given a specific deadline when her permit application will be either granted or denied; and the applicant must be given an opportunity for review of any denial before a neutral magistrate.[179] Although these cases concerned First Amendment activities such as the showing of films or the holding of protest marches, the Court made clear that these requirements apply to any law that "makes the peaceful enjoyment of *freedoms which the Constitution guarantees* contingent upon" the acquisition of a license or permit.[180]

State and local governments, however, routinely ignore these safeguards, imposing licensing and permit requirements that condition permits on vague criteria such as "good cause," or even subjective aesthetic criteria (as in the case of architectural design review for building permits[181]), and engaging in interminable delays that end up depriving applicants of either their permits or an opportunity for judicial review.[182] What's

---

178. *See, e.g.*, State v. Moore, 376 S.E.2d 877, 879 (Ga. 1989); State v. Austin, 704 P.2d 55, 59 (1985); Waller v. State Const. Indus. Licensing Bd., 299 S.E.2d 554, 555–56 (Ga. 1983); Heritage Vill. Church & Missionary Fellowship, Inc. v. State, 253 S.E.2d 473, 484 (N.C. App. 1979), *aff'd*, 263 S.E.2d 726 (N.C. 1980); Katzev v. Los Angeles Cnty., 341 P.2d 310, 316 (Cal. 1959); City of Mt. Vernon v. Julian, 17 N.E.2d 52, 55 (Ill. 1938).

179. Freedman v. State of Md., 380 U.S. 51, 58–59 (1965). *See also* FW/PBS, Inc. v. City of Dallas, 493 U.S. 215, 227–28 (1990).

180. Staub v. City of Baxley, 355 U.S. 313, 322 (1958) (emphasis added).

181. *See, e.g.*, Burns v. Town of Palm Beach, 999 F.3d 1317 (11th Cir. 2021), *cert. denied*, 142 S. Ct. 1361 (2022).

182. Consider, for example, *Lewis v. Carrano*, 844 F. Supp. 2d 325 (E.D.N.Y. 2012), in which the property owner applied for a permit in 2007. In 2010, when he had still received no answer, he sued on the

more, applicants who seek to appeal a denial are often forced into an administrative review process where the rules of procedure and evidence that govern courts do not apply.

This is an issue ripe for legal challenge. The U.S. Supreme Court recently expressed concern about the vagueness of a New York licensing statute predicated on "proper cause,"[183] and state courts have often expressed similar concerns.[184] One obstacle is that some courts have been reluctant to apply the void for vagueness principle in the business context, on the theory that businesses can afford legal representation to advise them on the meaning of statutes.[185] Whatever merit this view may have with respect to big businesses, however, it surely does not apply to an entrepreneur trying to figure out what does and does not entitle him to a license. And in any event, as Justice Gorsuch has observed, there's little rationality in requiring some laws to meet a minimal standard of clarity while allowing other laws to fall below that threshold, even though they can carry equally stringent penalties: "Why, for example, would due process require [the legislature] to speak more clearly when it seeks to deport a lawfully resident alien than when it wishes to subject a citizen to indefinite civil commitment, strip him of a business license essential to his family's living, or confiscate his home? I can think of no good answer."[186]

In 2023, Arizona adopted legislation drafted by the Goldwater Institute that requires state and local governments to comply with the clarity and time-limit requirements the U.S. Supreme Court's precedents already mandate. Other states should adopt similar legislation—applicable to all permit requirements that govern any constitutionally

---

grounds that the government's refusal to act on his permit application deprived him of his constitutional rights. Amazingly, the court found the case unripe, with the self-contradictory conclusion that "[s]ince plaintiff's claim arises from the delay in issuing the wetlands permit, there must be a final decision with respect to the wetlands permit" before he could sue. *Id.* at 330–31.

183. New York State Rifle & Pistol Ass'n, Inc. v. Bruen, 142 S. Ct. 2111, 2156 (2022).

184. *See, e.g.*, Squire Rest. & Lounge, Inc. v. City & Cnty. of Denver, 890 P.2d 164, 166–67 (Colo. App. 1994); City of Miami v. Save Brickell Ave., Inc., 426 So. 2d 1100, 1105 (Fla. Dist. Ct. App. 1983); Waterfront Ests. Dev., Inc. v. City of Palos Hills, 597 N.E.2d 641, 648–49 (Ill. Ct. App. 1992); Mini Mart, Inc. v. City of Minot, 347 N.W.2d 131 (N.D. 1984).

185. *See, e.g.*, Banks v. Spirit Aerosystems Inc., 457 P.3d 213 (Kan. Ct. App. 2020); Massachusetts Fed'n of Tchrs., AFT, AFL-CIO v. Bd. of Educ., 767 N.E.2d 549, 564 (Mass. 2002).

186. Sessions v. Dimaya, 138 S. Ct. 1204, 1231 (2018) (Gorsuch, J., concurring).

protected activity—to ensure that permit requirements are brought in line with basic principles of due process.

CONCLUSION

State constitutions offer many opportunities for advancing the cause of economic freedom. Taking this route involves some unique challenges—but also unique advantages. Litigators should promote economic freedom in state courts—and state judges should protect this freedom more vigorously than federal courts do.

Unenumerated Stories: Tales of How Unenumerated Rights Furthered Economic Liberty

By Anthony B. Sanders*

am delighted to lend my thoughts to Cato's symposium on restoring economic liberty. My contribution humbly adds three points. First, to briefly explain (not at all for the first time) that a large part of the challenge with vindicating economic liberty in court is that it is usually protected as an unenumerated right. Second, to focus on a species of constitutional language I have written about elsewhere through which economic liberty's unenumerated status becomes less mysterious and more comfortable: "Baby Ninth Amendments." Third, to illustrate how these "Baby Ninths" can protect economic liberty in the future by telling a few tales about how they actually have protected it in the past. My hope is readers, after hearing these stories, will be less afraid of unenumerated rights and more confident of their normality in restoring economic liberty.

My first two points are heavily interrelated, so I will weave them together in the next section. After that we will get to storytelling.

I. UNENUMERATED PATHWAYS

Why don't courts protect economic liberty? Is it a love of central economic planning? An extreme reluctance to "second-guess" legislatures? The haunting of *Lochner*'s ghost? Is economic liberty simply an innocent bystander knocked down like Mrs. Palsgraf in a

---

* Director of the Center for Judicial Engagement at the Institute for Justice.

35

conservative stampede away from "the right to privacy"? Like many things in life and law, there is no one correct, monocausal, answer. All of these suggestions are, by some measure, true. They are all—to some extent—*the* reason why, in modern times, state and federal courts generally do not declare unconstitutional various denials of economic liberty. Therefore, I do not mean to suggest that *the* reason I am about to discuss is the *only* reason for economic liberty's redheaded stepchild status and that if this problem could be solved, then courts would automatically knock down unreasonable barriers to trade in the marketplace.

But my reason is, nevertheless, a big one. It is our old friend unenumerated rights. When it comes to the U.S. Constitution, economic liberty is not enumerated. Sure, there are caveats to this. There is the Contracts Clause. It is most assertedly enumerated and still not taken all that seriously.[1] The same can be said for many applications of the Takings Clause, which I see as a species of economic liberty protection.[2] There are also (much) narrower slivers of explicit protection of economic liberty in the U.S. Constitution such as the Tonnage Clause and the (nonoperative these days) Gold Clauses. The right to earn a living *itself*, though? We must find it elsewhere in the Constitution via some implication such as a due process clause or the Privileges or Immunities Clause.

I will admit that, alternatively, one could forget the Constitution's text altogether and just go full natural rights. To this I say, good luck. Under current constitutional jurisprudence it is definitely not enough to simply walk into court and say, "This statute violates my rights, although these particular rights are not connected at all to the text of the Constitution." No federal judge is going to help you, positivist or not. Therefore, unenumerated—but nevertheless, *constitutionally protected*—rights are what we are left with.

It was the centrality of unenumerated rights to the economic liberty enterprise that led me to write *Baby Ninth Amendments: How Americans Embraced Unenumerated Rights and Why It Matters*.[3] Enumerated rights are scarce. Unenumerated rights are, as a

---

1. Arguably the greatest-ever champion of judicial restraint, the late Lino Graglia, admitted that when the Supreme Court refused to take the Contracts Clause seriously in *Home Building & Loan Assoc. v. Blaisdell*, 46 U.S. 398 (1934), it upheld "perhaps the most clearly unconstitutional law to come to the Court in its history." Lino A. Graglia, *The Burger Court and Economic Rights*, 33 TULSA L.J. 41, 48 (1997).

2. *See, e.g.*, Kelo v. City of New London, 545 U.S. 469 (2005).

3. University of Michigan Press (2023) (hereafter SANDERS, BABY NINTHS).

delegate to the 1850–51 Maryland Constitutional Convention said, "very numerous."[4] After all, that is a reason why judges and others shy away from them. As I hear from skeptics over and over again, if we do not have some "limiting principle," judges will just start making up rights willy-nilly.

What is not understood by many judges or most anyone else is that not only are unenumerated rights *themselves* "very numerous," but so are unenumerated rights *clauses*. This is not widely known because of our legal culture's focus on the U.S. Constitution, which has, basically, only three possible textual hooks to protect unenumerated rights: the Privileges or Immunities Clause, the Ninth Amendment, and the due process clauses. If we look at state constitutions, however, we see many more. As I detail in the book, there are 33 states that have "Baby Ninth Amendments," state versions of the Ninth Amendment. Well over 30 state constitutions (the exact number depends on how you classify them) have "Lockean Natural Rights Guarantees," broad protections of various rights such as "liberty" and "the pursuit of happiness."[5] Then there are, as in the U.S. Constitution, state due process clauses and law of the land clauses (the two are considered interchangeable). In short, language that looks like it protects unenumerated rights is not unusual. It is common. And, as I argue in the book, this commonness demonstrates that unenumerated rights are not weird. In fact, they are *popular*. Thus, it should not be controversial for an entrepreneur to invoke economic liberty as an unenumerated right in state court. It is something that her state constitution is *designed* to protect. This is not a matter of judges "making stuff up." It is judges simply enforcing constitutional text.

Even so, lawyers and judges are so used to our reluctance to effectuate actual constitutional text when it comes to unenumerated rights that pure textualism and logic is not enough. And this space is not the place for it. I will not belabor here all the history and legal theory that I bring to bear in my book to support these assertions. Instead, I am going to provide something else, something that all humans yearn for: stories. I want to tell the tales of how judges enforcing unenumerated rights—specifically, the

4. 1 DEBATES AND PROCEEDINGS OF THE MARYLAND REFORM CONSTITUTIONAL CONVENTION 225 (1851) (remarks of Delegate Parke on his proposed Baby Ninth Amendment to add to the Maryland Declaration of Rights).

5. One count puts the number as high as 39 states. Steven G. Calabresi, et al., *Individual Rights under State Constitution in 2018: What Rights Are Deeply Rooted in a Modern-Day Consensus of the States?*, 94 NOTRE DAME L. REV. 49, 125 (2018).

unenumerated right of economic liberty via a Baby Ninth Amendment—have protected real people with real problems. These stories come from cases that I discuss in my book but that I did not detail to a significant degree. Here I go deeper into their history and explain how the unenumerated right of economic liberty, protected by constitutional language specifically designed to protect unenumerated rights, protected those people.[6]

What you will learn from these stories is that the courts involved protected a right even though it was not enumerated, prevented the state or local government from interfering with the person's economic choices, and (most importantly) this all seemed very ordinary. Just like in numerous other civil liberties cases, the government continued enforcing other laws protecting public health and safety even though the court commanded "stop" in this particular instance. These stories help demonstrate that we can protect unenumerated rights—including economic liberty—while continuing to let the rest of the government function. If any judges need courage to enforce the right of economic liberty, my hope is they can draw it from these stories.

II. HOW COURTS HAVE PROTECTED ECONOMIC LIBERTY VIA BABY NINTH AMENDMENTS

A. I Challenge Thee to a Duel!

Today a challenge to a duel generally elicits rounds of laughter. At most, the minds of modern Americans might wander to the Hamilton-Burr affair, and if they are of a certain age, to the declaration that "I am not throwin' away my shot."

So it is a little odd that one of the most detailed and far-ranging cases about natural rights and natural justice in U.S. history concerned the right to not take a pledge about dueling. And yet it did. What was this firestorm of legal exposition in 1838 Alabama, and why did it make such a big deal about a lawyer pledging he had not fought "in single combat or otherwise, with any deadly weapon"?

I discuss what we know here about this matter, *In re Dorsey*.[7] But some things will remain mysterious when we explore this mysterious case—the first case to use a Baby

---

6. Although they are not in the book, I published earlier versions of these stories on the Center for Judicial Engagement's blog. *See* https://ij.org/center-for-judicial-engagement/center-for-judicial -engagement-blog/.

7. 7 Port. 293 (Ala. 1838).

Ninth Amendment in a judicial opinion. Thus, to round things out, we will also talk a bit about dueling and what it meant in the early history of our country. It may seem odd to focus on dueling in a piece about economic liberty, but in many other ways this story is a precursor to so many instances of occupational licensing we have today.

The facts of the case are pretty sparse. John L. Dorsey wanted to be admitted to the Alabama bar. He objected, however, to taking a required oath. The state legislature had mandated the oath in 1826. It was required not just of Alabama elected and appointed officials, but also of all licensed attorneys of any kind. It read:

I do solemnly swear that I have neither directly nor indirectly given, accepted, or knowingly carried a challenge, In writing or otherwise, to any person or persons, (being a citizen of this State,) to fight in single combat or otherwise, with any deadly weapon, either in or out of this State, or aided or abetted in the same, since the first day of January, one thousand eight hundred and twenty-six; and that I will neither directly nor indirectly, give[,] accept, or knowingly carry a challenge in any manner whatsoever, to any person or persons, (being a citizen of this State,) to fight in single combat or otherwise, with any deadly weapon, either in or out of this State, or in any manner aid or abet the same, during the time for which I am elected, or during the time of my continuance in office, or during the time of my continuance in the discharge of any public function.[8]

Dorsey filed a motion to be admitted to the bar without having to take the oath.[9] It is hard to tell from the opinion, but it appears he filed it in the state supreme court itself. He made a number of constitutional challenges to the oath requirement, invoking all manner of legal authorities: from Lord Coke to Magna Carta, to various decisions of other state supreme courts, to a slew of provisions of Alabama's bill of rights. Included among these was Alabama's Baby Ninth Amendment, which at the time said, "[T]his enumeration of certain rights shall not be construed to deny or disparage others retained by the people."[10]

8. *Id.* at 355 (as quoted by the court).

9. *Id.* at 293.

10. ALA. CONST. of 1819, art. I, § 30; *In re Dorsey*, 7 Port. at 377.

Dorsey prevailed by a vote of 2–1, with the majority declaring the law unconstitutional and void, meaning Dorsey could become a licensed Alabama lawyer without taking the oath. Although two justices voted in his favor, they each wrote separately with slightly different reasoning.

All three opinions in the case are truly amazing works of legal reasoning and rhetoric of their time. Fans of Lord Coke will be tickled by the citations to Bonham's Case.[11] There is also a discussion of the 1798 U.S. Supreme Court case *Calder v. Bull*[12] and the "dueling" arguments over natural justice by Justices Chase and Iredell.[13]

How do the opinions tie in to the Baby Ninth? In my book I explain how each of the three opinions discusses the Baby Ninth in a way that implies it recognizes rights beyond those enumerated in the Alabama Constitution, and that those "others retained by the people" are judicially enforceable.[14] That is something on which all the judges agree. And that is a big deal, as again, it was the first judicial opinion in American history to interpret a Baby Ninth.

But how the Baby Ninth and the various other provisions in the Alabama Constitution at issue actually protect Dorsey from having to take the duel oath is a bit hard to follow, to be honest. It seems there is a strong reaction against the oath requiring someone to swear they had not done something in the past.[15] Perhaps long in the past before the applicant even thought of becoming a lawyer. In a way, it was seen as an ex post facto law. The judges also point out that the Alabama Constitution specifically allows for the legislature to address the problem of dueling, but not in this way.[16] Thus, there is an enumerated powers-type argument, which you would expect more in conjunction with the U.S. Constitution. (In the book, I address how this was a common, though not ubiquitous, way of viewing state powers in the nineteenth century.) In addition, one judge was particularly concerned that the question as to whether an oath taker had

---

11. *See In re Dorsey*, 7 Port. at 375 (opinion of Ormond, J.); *see also id.* at 415 (Collier, C. J., dissenting) (distinguishing *Bonham's Case* as against the tide of English jurisprudence).

12. 3 U.S. (3 Dall.) 386 (1798).

13. *Id.* at 375–76 (opinion of Ormand, J.).

14. SANDERS, BABY NINTHS at 57–59.

15. *See In re Dorsey*, 7 Port. at 359 (opinion of Goldthwaite, J.).

16. *Id.* at 363 (opinion of Goldthwaite, J.); *id* at 371 (opinion of Ormand, J.).

engaged in a duel was not to be found by a jury but instead was essentially to be extracted from him. It was almost as if the oath taker is being forced to testify against himself.[17]

The dissent, on the other hand, saw the oath as a pretty straightforward character qualification, like a background check today.[18] In contrast, the majority judges said it is fine to take a lawyer's license away if they committed an illegal act, such as engaging in a duel, while practicing law. It was the extreme, retroactive effect of the oath that was so disconcerting. Maybe one way to think about it is that the oath requirement was akin to laws today that bar someone who has done something wrong in the past from employment in the future, even when that wrong was a long time ago and the applicant has been reformed.

Still, even if today we might sympathize with Mr. Dorsey about the reach deep into his past, it seems odd from our perspective that such a big deal was made about an oath about dueling, of all things. To us, dueling is akin to attempted murder (even if "consensual attempted murder"). Lawyers can get barred from the bar for all kinds of past bad acts, many arguably not nearly as bad as dueling, such as embezzlement. Why was all this legal reasoning and rhetoric spilled on such an odd provision? And what was Mr. Dorsey's story, anyway?

First let's talk about dueling, and then what we know about Dorsey.

Dueling is a fascinating aspect of early American culture. Various restrictions and bans on dueling were common in the early United States, including in state constitutions themselves.[19] But these laws were often quite ineffective. Dueling was a widespread practice, especially among "gentlemen," when honor or family, or both, were threatened.[20]

And because it was so common among "gentlemen"—that is, what today we might call the upper-middle classes—it, of course, was common among applicants to the bar. These applicants were relatively young men who may or may not have recently been involved in spats involving their and their family's reputations. And since dueling was, in

17. *Id.* at 368 (opinion of Goldthwaite, J.).

18. *Id.* at 419 (Collier, C. J., dissenting).

19. *See, e.g.*, MISS. CONST. of 1817, art. VI, § 2; TENN. CONST. of 1834, art. 9, § 3.

20. *See generally* Alison L. LaCroix, *To Gain the Whole World and Lose His Own Soul: Nineteenth-Century American Dueling as Public Law and Private Code*, 33 HOFSTRA L. REV. 501 (2004).

a sense, a "victimless crime" (or at least a crime where the victim opts into the crime), it was hard to police. Consider a modern parallel: Just as laws barring young people who have ever used illegal drugs from certain jobs are seen as overbroad today, a bar on anyone who had ever participated in a duel might have been seen the same way in 1838. I am not saying dueling was the marijuana of the 1830s, but it was similarly popular in relevant circles. (Plus, since dueling was not something that the working class and the poor were involved with in the same way, there was not the same disparity of treatment between "elite" offenders and others that we have with the modern drug war.) The judges in the *In re Dorsey* majority may have seen themselves as having to police the vast numbers of otherwise "respectable" young men who were put in the position of either lying or forgoing a career in law because of a common "youthful indiscretion."

As for Mr. Dorsey himself, we sadly know very little. The reported opinions tell us almost nothing about him other than his name, that he filed the motion, and that he argued the case pro se (his argument and his opponent's are included in the case reporter). Whatever the story is, he knew enough to invoke his state's Baby Ninth, a few other parts of its constitution, and a great many sources. Whether he actually had participated in a duel in his younger days and did not want that becoming more widely known we do not know. But it would not be a surprise.

B. Frugal Freedoms

Charging too little is not a complaint you hear from many customers. Have you ever sat for a haircut, or picked up your laundry, and demanded to pay the barber or cleaner more than they asked for? Yeah, me neither. Amazingly, though, sometimes the government passes *laws* requiring those same businesses to charge you more.

Actually, it is not amazing at all when you learn those laws are enacted at the behest of established companies who do not like the competition. "Ruinous competition," so they claim.

These laws still exist even in today's enlightened times, especially in certain industries such as transportation.[21] At one point they were even more common, most notoriously

---

21. *See, e.g.*, Mark W. Frankena, *Nashville's Anti-Competitive "Black-Car" Regulations*, REGULATION, Summer 2013, at 14, 16.

in the Great Depression when the Roosevelt administration sought to divide U.S. indus-try into price-controlled cartels.[22]

But the federal government was not the only one enforcing minimum prices during the New Deal. Take Mobile, Alabama, where a barber and a cleaner needed some help in providing lower prices to their customers. They got that help partly from Alabama's Baby Ninth Amendment.

Pat Rouse ran a barbershop in Mobile. One day, upon offering a service, likely a hair-cut (it is unknown how good it was), the city cited him for violating an ordinance man-dating a minimum price.[23] Meanwhile, somewhere else in town, A. E. Gibson was in the laundry business and "accepted for pressing and cleaning, and did press and clean a suit of men's clothes for the charge of fifty cents," which was less than the ordinance al-lowed.[24] In the spirit of good uses of government power, the city issued Mr. Gibson a citation as well.

At trial, both men argued that the law violated various provisions of the Alabama Con-stitution and the Fourteenth Amendment to the U.S. Constitution.[25] The trial court agreed, ruling the ordinance unconstitutional. The city appealed and lost again at the intermediate court of appeals. The case then went to the state supreme court, which essentially framed the issue as whether it was constitutional for the government to impose a minimum price "in an inherently lawful occupation."[26]

What did that last phrase mean? Essentially, an occupation that is commonly prac-ticed and is not "affected by a public interest."[27] Courts had already said at the time that governments had some leeway in setting minimum prices to protect "ruinous competi-tion" in certain sensitive areas, especially capital-intensive areas such as railroads. Some courts, most prominently the U.S. Supreme Court in the 1934 case *Nebbia v. New York*,[28]

---

22. *See* A.L.A. Schechter Poultry Corp. v. United States, 295 U.S. 495, 520–27 (1935).

23. City of Mobile v. Rouse, 173 So. 266 (Ala. 1937) ("*Rouse II*").

24. *Id.*

25. City of Mobile v. Rouse, 173 So. 254, 257 (Ala. Ct. App. 1937) ("*Rouse I*").

26. *Rouse II*, 173 So. at 267.

27. *Id.*

28. 291 U.S. 502 (1934).

had cast aside that distinction, making it much easier for the government to regulate prices in any kind of industry. But to the Alabama court in 1937, that distinction still held. Otherwise, explained the court, the justification for meddling with the freedom to set prices knew no bounds.

The court swiftly found that the justification of protecting established businesses from ruinous competition did not justify restricting Rouse and Gibson from charging their customers cheaper prices. The ruling was broad, invoking the Fourteenth Amendment and quoting from the expansive language of *Meyer v. Nebraska*.[29] But it also used Alabama's Baby Ninth Amendment.

Similar to the earlier version we saw in *In re Dorsey*, the state's Baby Ninth is the first sentence of Section 36 of the state's declaration of rights:

> That this enumeration of certain rights shall not impair or deny others retained by the people; and, to guard against any encroachments on the rights herein retained, we declare that everything in this declaration of rights is excepted out of the general powers of government, and shall forever remain inviolate.

The Baby Ninth part of this refers to "others," other rights that are not enumerated in the constitution but that, the court explained, are not given over to the government but retained by the people and *also* protected by the constitution. Since the right to work an inherently lawful occupation was one of the "others" "retained," the court said this arbitrary restriction on working such an occupation was unconstitutional.

That is the Baby Ninth. But let's dwell for a moment on the second half of Section 36— that is, everything after the semicolon. In my book I describe it as a "Baby Tenth."[30] Originally inspired by the Tenth Amendment when the first version was drafted in Pennsylvania in December 1789, it refers to the powers that the people delegate to the government. Unlike with the federal government, however, to which the people delegate *enumerated* powers, here the people have delegated *general* powers. This is in keeping with the standard understanding of the powers that state governments have. Today we would call these general powers the "police power."

---

29. 262 U.S. 390 (1923) (quoted by *Rouse II*, 173 So. at 268).

30. SANDERS, BABY NINTHS at 27–30.

But note that "the people" who adopted this language were a bit nervous about these "general powers of government." The Baby Tenth recognizes that there can be "encroachments" on rights, specifically "the rights herein retained." And to guard against that, "everything in this declaration of rights"—both enumerated rights earlier in the declaration and these unenumerated "retained" rights—are "excepted out" of the state's powers and even "remain inviolate" forever. It is almost as though the constitution recognizes that the government is a dangerous animal and has to be kept on a short leash. It is important to understand that this constrained view of the police power can go hand in hand with constitutional rights. One is the flip side of the other. Victories for economic liberty are great from a rights perspective, but they can be just as meaningful from a limited police power perspective as well.

Pat Rouse and A. E. Gibson, presumably, were able to go on charging their customers prices that their customers preferred after this ruling. The reasoning did not spread any higher, however. Just days after the Alabama Supreme Court's opinion came out, the U.S. Supreme Court made its famous "switch in time," junking both the doctrine of enumerated powers and the limits on the police power under the Fourteenth Amendment that Alabama's Baby Ninth was a cousin of.[31] In the future, litigants increasingly only had state constitutions to protect their economic liberty. And even then, the results were increasingly worse.

But maybe things can change in that regard. After all, as I explain in the book, two-thirds of all states explicitly recognize rights "retained by the people." We simply need judges to read those constitutions, like the one in *City of Mobile v. Rouse*, including front-end limitations on powers, not just back-end limitations for rights. And isn't that something judges should be doing these days since "we're all textualists now"?

C. Educational Entrepreneurs

Have you ever seen the right "to build a private school on residential property and educate children in it" in a constitution? No? That is because no such explicit constitutional right exists. It is a pretty specific use of one's property and liberty. Not the kind of thing a delegate to a constitutional convention would propose to enumerate.

---

31. *See* W. Coast Hotel v. Parrish, 300 U.S. 379 (1937) (state police powers); NLRB v. Jones & Laughlin Steel Corp., 301 U.S. 1 (1937) (enumerated powers).

It sounds kind of important, though, right? If you are going to start a school you need to put it somewhere. And, yes, you could put it on commercial property, but if you want children to walk or bike to school and breathe clean air while playing outside, it is much better to have it in a neighborhood. That is where public elementary schools are all the time, and for good reason.

Private schools can be run to make money, but most are nonprofit, at least in name. But whether a school primarily exists to acquire cash or as a venture that furthers other values of the Founders, the enterprise of private education is closely tied to economic liberty. It is a service provided to customers that—as advocates for school choice know very well—is responsive to consumer (i.e., parental) demand. Therefore, although you might technically argue that when the Oregon Supreme Court recognized a right to start a school in a residential neighborhood in 1932 the court was not protecting "economic liberty," it certainly was furthering the right to pursue a calling and the right to be an entrepreneur. For that reason, it is a good example for this essay.

Oregon in the 1920s was not a great environment to open a private school, particularly if you were Catholic. In 1922, the state's voters approved a law that banned the private schooling of elementary-aged children. Heavily backed by the Ku Klux Klan, the measure tapped into the anti-immigrant and anti-Catholic hysteria of the post–Great War years.[32] The Society of Sisters—a Catholic organization that ran a number of affected schools—and another private school, Hill Military Academy, challenged the law. And in 1925, the Supreme Court found the ban unconstitutional because it violated the right of the schools to contract with the parents to educate their children and the right of the parents to direct that education.[33]

That may have saved the Academy and the Society's schools, but it unfortunately did not end up being enough for another group. In a newly developed area of Portland, All Saints Parish had purchased some adjacent lots in 1914 and built a church on one of them in 1917.[34] The parish also wanted to eventually build a school on two of the other lots.[35]

32. *See* Paula Abrams, *The Little Red Schoolhouse: Pierce, State Monopoly of Education and the Politics of Intolerance*, 20 CONST. COMM. 61, 66–70 (2003).

33. Pierce v. Soc'y of Sisters, 268 U.S. 510 (1925).

34. Roman Catholic Archbishop v. Baker, 15 P.2d 391, 392 (Or. 1932).

35. *Id.*

After the *Pierce* case cleared the way, the parish moved forward with those plans. But then another kind of restriction on constitutional rights stepped forward: zoning.

Following the new nationwide trend of central planning, the voters of Portland adopted a zoning ordinance in 1924.[36] Like most any zoning ordinance, it split the city into various districts where only certain kinds of land uses were allowed. The church and adjacent lots were in the typically most restrictive kind of district: single family.[37]

The ordinance only allowed a limited set of buildings in the single-family district by right. A property owner could build other kinds through a rezoning process. But this required permission of the city council and the sign-off of over 50 percent of all neighbors within 100 feet of the property.[38]

The parish went to the city council, which investigated the proposal and to their credit, initially voted in favor of the plan.[39] However, some of the neighbors then filed objections, and the council, in compliance with the 50 percent requirement of the ordinance, ultimately voted no.[40] The parish then went to state court, arguing that the prohibition on running the school on its lots violated various provisions of the U.S. and Oregon Constitutions. The plaintiffs won in the trial court and the case then went to the Oregon Supreme Court.

What objections did those neighbors have to the school? For anyone familiar with today's battles between NIMBYs and YIMBYs, the arguments look all too familiar. They came down to property values, traffic, and noise. Yet, instead of reflexively deferring to those arguments—as often happens today—the court seriously examined them, finding them spurious. Regarding property values, the court said:

> It is also contended that the erection of a school on this site will lessen the value of the property of many of the adjacent property owners, many of whom bought their property and built a mansion thereon for a home, after the passage of the ordinance, and spent large sums of money in making lawns and setting out shrubbery.

36. *Id.* at 391.
37. *Id.* at 391–92.
38. *Id.* at 394.
39. *Id.* at 392–93.
40. *Id.* at 393.

The reasons given for this decrease in value will apply with equal force to any other residential district, either of the first or second class.[41]

In other words, the court recognized that this argument could be made about essentially any school—or other building—anywhere.

And regarding traffic and noise, the court was incredulous. It is worth quoting a chunk of the opinion on that:

They complain that it will be dangerous for the children to cross those through streets. That matter may be easily remedied by compelling vehicular traffic to slow down at a designated crossing.

There is no virtue in the argument that the children will trespass upon private property within the vicinity of the school. There is a sufficient remedy at law to prevent such a trespass.

Then *they complain of the noise that the children will make.* There is a double-track street car line on one of the adjacent streets. These cars in their operation are not noiseless. They are run "from early morn to dewy eve and far into the night"; they pass and repass many times every hour.

There are also in the vicinity two through streets, carrying much vehicular traffic. Automobiles, whether truck or passenger, in operation are not silent. These are driven over those streets at all times of the day and night. The school children will be at play probably a few minutes before 9 o'clock in the morning, when school takes up, and during short intermissions (usually ten minutes in length), one in the forenoon and one in the afternoon, all taking place between 8:45 a.m. and 3:30 p.m. *It appears that the noises made by street cars and automobiles are preferable to the prattle and laughter and merry shouts of the children of a primary school*—"the playful children just let loose from school." We agree with counsel for defendants that children at play make more or less noise. Children were ever so. They were so nearly 2,000 years ago, when a man, who was not born in a mansion but in a manger, said, "Suffer little children, and forbid them not to come unto me; for of such is the kingdom of heaven."[42]

---

41. *Id.* at 394.

42. *Id.* at 394–95 (emphasis added).

The court even quoted from the then recent case where the U.S. Supreme Court had blessed zoning, *Village of Euclid v. Ambler Realty Co.*,[43] and said while *Euclid* held zoning generally constitutional, specific cases can be unreasonable and therefore invalid. If only zoning litigation were more that way today.[44]

On the legal specifics of the ruling, the court cited federal and state precedents, but also to *both* Oregon's Baby Ninth Amendment and the actual Ninth Amendment. Oregon's version states, "This enumeration of rights[] and privileges shall not be construed to impair or deny others retained by the people."[45] What rights had Portland violated in the case? Essentially, the right I identified above, but framed as follows:

> The right to own property is an inherent right, one of those rights with which men "are endowed by their Creator." This right of ownership is subject to the superior rights of the public to appropriate such property for certain public uses on payment of just compensation. The right to own carries with it the right to use that property in any manner that the owner may desire so long as such use will not impair the public health, peace, safety, or general welfare. The kind of school proposed to be erected, will not interfere with the public health; it cannot affect the public peace; it surely will not endanger the public safety; and by all civilized peoples, an educational institution, whose curriculum complies with the state law, is considered an aid to the general welfare.[46]

What did this result mean for All Saints Parish? According to a history published upon the parish's 75th anniversary, the parish moved forward with construction and, staffed by the Sisters of the Holy Names of Jesus and Mary, opened its doors to about 125 students in 1936.[47] Since then it has been through many expansions and today teaches a

---

43. 272 U.S. 365 (1926).

44. After *Euclid*, the deference paid to zoning laws got progressively even more deferential, culminating in the extreme capitulation of *Village of Belle Terre v. Boraas*, 416 U.S. 1, 9 (1974) ("A quiet place where yards are wide, people few, and motor vehicles restricted are legitimate guidelines in a land-use project addressed to family needs.").

45. OR. CONST. art 1, § 33.

46. *Baker*, 15 P.2d at 395.

47. *A Community of Saints: The History of All Saints Parish 1917–1992*, https://files.ecatholic.com/13217/documents/2016/10/SKM_C654e16102711080.pdf.

student body of about 200 children from pre-K through eighth grade.[48] Since the Oregon Supreme Court—and the U.S. Supreme Court—found the various attempts to prevent it from operating to be unconstitutional, it has educated thousands of children whose parents chose to send them there over other options. And it has employed many adults, who work there to pursue their calling as teachers.

What allowed all of this choice and learning? Many people and many efforts. But one of them was judges taking unenumerated rights seriously, thanks in part to Oregon's Baby Ninth Amendment.

D. Grapes of Wrath

"Upon this appeal, the facts as alleged in the complaint and as disclosed by such records must be accepted as true. The story so told reads like a sequel to Steinbeck's 'The Grapes of Wrath.'"[49]

With these lines in its opening paragraph, you would expect the Minnesota Supreme Court to be winding up for something special. And *Thiede v. Town of Scandia Valley* (1944) did not disappoint. Along the way, it set down one of the strongest precedents for unenumerated rights in Minnesota's history, if not America's. It is not quite the epic of the Joad family,[50] but one might argue it stands as a better story because (1) it really happened and (2) it is much more sympathetic to the American free market tradition than Steinbeck's epic. It concerns town officials throwing a family out of their home in the depths of a northern Minnesota winter—a family that had fallen on hard times but was exercising its economic liberty and simply wanted to be left alone. And to top it all off, after finishing my book, I learned the tale had a happy ending beyond the court's ruling.

The story begins in the depths of the Great Depression. Children of families who had immigrated to the Upper Midwest, Louis Thiede and Louise Harbeke married in 1930 and for several years tried scratching out a living farming in eastern North Dakota.[51] In March 1935, with little kids in tow, they moved to central Minnesota. There they bounced

48. According to its website, https://allsaintsportland.com.

49. Thiede v. Town of Scandia Valley, 14 N.W.2d 400, 402 (Minn. 1944).

50. JOHN STEINBECK, THE GRAPES OF WRATH (1939).

51. In addition to the Minnesota Supreme Court's opinion, sources for some of the biographical specifics in this narrative are my conversation with Paul Thiede and details found on Ancestry.com drawn from various U.S. Census records and other public documents available there.

around a bit, living in a couple of towns in Todd County, including Fawn Lake, and also living at times in Scandia Valley in nearby Morrison County. In October 1938, they moved back to Scandia Valley and stayed there through the time of the court case. In fact, in 1939 they purchased a 40-acre tract and built a small house. That was their home when the legal controversies arose. These different counties and the frequent moves would become bizarrely consequential.

Beginning in December 1936, the Thiedes intermittently received poor relief from both counties at various times. "[S]urplus commodities" was how the court described it,[52] which likely meant they accepted food when they did not have anything for themselves. In addition, Mr. Thiede worked for the WPA at times for a few years and received some earnings.[53]

Due to the way Minnesota's poor-relief laws were written, the Thiedes' frequent moves coupled with their decision to take relief made things bureaucratically complicated for the local officials in charge of their relief. Essentially, a family was only supposed to receive relief from a jurisdiction if they had lived there for a year before going on relief. Through the quirks of their moves, this happened to be Fawn Lake.

In 1942, even though they had been in Scandia Valley for four years and (it appears from the opinion) even though they had not received any relief from Fawn Lake in about three years, "a dispute arose between the towns of Scandia Valley and Fawn Lake as to the legal settlement of the Thiede family."[54] The towns actually went to court to figure this out.[55] Meanwhile, the Thiedes completely stopped receiving any kind of poor relief. Nevertheless, the dispute continued and eventually Fawn Lake gave notice to Scandia Valley that it was terminating its responsibility to provide for the Thiedes unless within 30 days they were removed from Scandia Valley and resettled in Fawn Lake. In other words, unless they voluntarily moved or were forced to.[56]

By the time this notice was given, in early 1943, the family had not taken a dime in relief from any arm of government for almost a year. So given that they were about to

---

52. *Thiede*, 14 N.W.2d at 403.

53. *Id.*

54. *Id.*

55. *Id.*

56. *Id.* at 404.

have lived in Scandia Valley without relief for long enough to have a new "legal settlement," it all sounds pretty technical, and nothing would happen. Right?

It turned out to be anything but technical. Upon receiving the notice from Fawn Lake, Scandia Valley officials sprang into action. They served their own notice on the family, ordering them to move to Fawn Lake within 10 days.[57] The family understandably refused to obey this, being that they were not on relief and, most importantly, owned their 40 acres free and clear, and by this time they had six children of various ages, all under 12.

But the town officials would not budge. They went to the county sheriff with an order requiring him to remove the family and their personal property. And so, he and a few minions did.

They did so, as Mrs. Thiede's complaint described, "with force and violence."[58] The sheriff even moved their livestock and farm machinery. The family and their belongings were dumped "in the farm yard of" Louis's mother in Fawn Lake.[59] It was late February and early March 1943. (It seems the job took the sheriff a few days.) The court describes it as "sub-zero" (Fahrenheit, of course). And a look at the historical weather data for Brainerd, Minnesota (only a few miles away) bears that out.[60] During that period the mercury fell below zero Fahrenheit several times, with a then record −24 degrees for March 2.

The sheriff and his personnel damaged the Thiedes' house and outbuildings. The family claimed they suffered from "extreme exposure" and "great mental anguish," among other injuries.[61] Funnily enough, the family moved back to their home only a few days later, perhaps after the sheriff and others had realized they had overacted and would not do it again. Not long after that, Mrs. Thiede took them and the town to court. The trial judge preliminarily ruled for her but certified the question for appeal to the state high court.

Thiede does not read like your average opinion, even your average victory for economic liberty or property rights. Outrage pours out of every word. Justice Thomas O. Streissguth, writing for a unanimous court, was angry and was not afraid to show it.

---

57. *Id.*

58. *Id.*

59. *Id.* at 404–05.

60. Obtained from the National Weather Service at https://www.weather.gov/wrh/Climate?wfo=dlh.

61. *Thiede*, 14 N.W.2d at 405.

He started his legal analysis with first principles: "The entire social and political structure of America rests upon the cornerstone that all men have certain rights which are inherent and inalienable."[62] What are those rights? He listed them broadly, and quoted Thomas Cooley's assertion that "[t]hese instruments measure the powers of rulers, but they do not measure the rights of the governed."[63] He noted that the Minnesota Constitution recognizes some rights but "does not attempt to enumerate" them all. Instead, it "significantly[] provides: 'The enumeration of rights in this constitution shall not be construed to deny or impair others retained by and inherent in the people' (Art. 1, § 16)."[64] That, as you might have guessed, is Minnesota's Baby Ninth Amendment, allowing the court to find a constitutional home for these "unmeasured" rights.

Justice Streissguth continued by stressing the age-old maxim that "[e]very man's house is his castle." It "is more than an epigram. It is a terse statement, in language which everyone should understand, of a legal concept older even than Magna Carta."[65] And from this and other sources, he concluded that the right to occupy one's freehold is a fundamental liberty. That right, he reasoned, cannot be taken away through the mere fact that a family has accepted relief in the past.

The opinion went on to discuss relief and the government's interests when providing it, but the bottom line was that the actions of the Scandia Valley officials, and the state statute they relied upon, were unconstitutional because they violated this basic right of occupying one's property.

Justice Streissguth also addressed the ability of Louise Thiede—the only named plaintiff—to sue for damages. The court said damages were available against the officials because they were not shielded with sovereign immunity. He even invoked Article I, Section 8 of the Minnesota Constitution, which guarantees that "[e]very person is entitled to a certain remedy in the laws for all injuries or wrongs which he may receive in his person, property, or character." "These words were not inserted in the constitution as a

---

62. *Id.*

63. *Id.* (citing THOMAS M. COOLEY, A TREATISE ON THE CONSTITUTIONAL LIMITATIONS WHICH REST UPON THE LEGISLATIVE POWER OF THE STATES OF THE AMERICAN UNION 95, 533 (Walter Carrington ed., 8th ed. 1927) (1868)).

64. *Id.*

65. *Id.*

matter of idle ceremony or as a 'string of generalities' . . . and must be respected even by public officers."[66]

I was unable to find out what happened in the litigation after the case was remanded. Perhaps it went to trial and no one appealed the judgment, or perhaps it settled. The *Minneapolis Star* (a paper that years later merged to form today's *Star Tribune*) thought the opinion a good drama, with the front-page headline "Evicted Family Wins 'Grapes of Wrath' Decision."[67]

What I was able to do, after my book had gone to press, is find out what happened to the family. The eight children (more were born after the lawsuit) went on to various successful endeavors after their modest beginnings. A number of them at one point worked for Northwest Airlines in different ways. And one of them, Paul Thiede, even served in the state legislature for a few terms after graduating from college and working as a journalist, and also served on his county board for 16 years.[68]

I reached out and briefly spoke to him when writing this story. I asked, among other things, if the *Grapes of Wrath* reference in the opinion was a bit overblown and whether the family was not actually that hard up. He said, though, that that characterization was not too far from the mark. He described his dad as a "rock farmer," just trying to scratch out a living for his family. Times were tough, especially during the Depression (before Paul was born), and even when he was growing up they lacked running water. Indeed, for him that was true all the way through high school. He also said that when he got to college a professor did not believe him when he wrote an essay about what it was like growing up.

Today the *Thiede* case stands as the clearest expression of almost any opinion about the American maxim that our constitutions do not explicitly contain all of our rights and that it is the job of the courts to protect all of our rights, whether explicitly or implicitly protected by our constitutions. It also makes for a firm statement of principle that our constitutions allow our courts to find government officials liable for damages when they violate those rights. We have cited *Thiede* a number of times in our cases at the Institute

---

66. *Id.* at 408 (quoting Rhodes v. Walsh, 57 N.W. 212, 213 (Minn. 1893)).

67. *Evicted Family Wins 'Grapes of Wrath' Decision*, MINNEAPOLIS STAR, Apr. 21, 1944, at 1.

68. Interview of Paul Thiede (May 2023); Thiede, Paul M., Minnesota Legislative Reference Library, https://www.lrl.mn.gov/legdb/fulldetail?id=10661.

for Justice. And we will continue to, especially when litigating those rights "retained by and inherent in the people" such as economic liberty.

CONCLUSION

The people in these stories were not seeking anything special or abnormal, let alone unsafe or socially poisonous. They just wanted to work as a lawyer, sell services for a cheaper price, educate children, and live and farm on their own property. To allow them to pursue those economic liberties, however, they had to rely on judges enforcing unenumerated rights. They won, and yet, by some miracle, the sky did not fall, children were not sent to workhouses, and the air was not polluted—but all were participants in the "parade of horribles" we will supposedly see with any kind of a return to the *Lochner* era." The track record is anything but that.

Americans have chosen to protect rights such as economic liberty, but they have generally done so in an unenumerated fashion. When courts honor this choice, ordinary people are allowed to do ordinary yet great things, such as lower prices, educate children, and pursue their callings. If more judges honored this choice of "unenumeration," we would have more of these ordinary things. That is, we would have more stories like those of John Dorsey, Pat Rouse, All Saints Parish, and Louis and Louise Thiede.

Nondelegation and the Right to Earn a Living: An Untapped Opportunity

By Ethan Blevins and Luke Wake*

INTRODUCTION

L itigators fighting for their clients' right to earn a living against occupational licensing and similar regulatory burdens should consider state nondelegation doctrines. These regulatory regimes are vulnerable to nondelegation challenge because—in many cases—state lawmakers have punted on important matters to state boards stacked with industry insiders. State licensing statutes often delegate capacious authority for these boards to decide fundamental policy like who qualifies for a license, what restrictions apply for licensed individuals, and what the scope of a licensed practice is.

In some cases, the statutes provide no governing standards at all. This conflicts with the foundational premise that in a free society, law must be set by our elected representatives.[1] Hence, even in states that follow the loose federal approach, there is room to invoke the nondelegation doctrine—even if only in pressing to constrain administrative discretion.

For that matter, we submit that occupational licensing regimes are uniquely vulnerable to nondelegation challenges because licensing boards are often comprised of

---

* Ethan Blevins is a constitutional law fellow with Pacific Legal Foundation. Luke Wake is a staff attorney with Pacific Legal Foundation.

1. Youngstown Sheet & Tube Co. v. Sawyer, 343 U.S. 579, 655 (1952) ("With all its defects, delays and inconveniences, men have discovered no technique for long preserving free government except that the executive be under the law, and that the law be made by parliamentary deliberations.").

members of the regulated profession. Because they have "skin in the game," there is heightened risk of unduly oppressive or protectionist regulation that may not reflect the public interest. And in many states this fact may have bearing on the nondelegation analysis, because the legislature should provide more definite governing standards when delegating rulemaking authority to a board that represents the special interests of a "faction."[2]

This article provides a roadmap for potential nondelegation challenges. We begin by discussing the similarities between the National Industrial Recovery Act's unlawful delegation of authority for the President to issue "industry codes" and the commonplace occupational licensing regime of the 21st century. Next, we discuss the state of nondelegation doctrine and explain why legislatures often cater to special interests through open-ended delegations. We then make a case that regulation promulgated by self-interested licensing boards may be vulnerable to challenge under various state nondelegation tests. We offer examples from Michigan, Montana, and Washington State.

But the ideas floated here could be applied in other states. Litigators should draw from persuasive authority in states with strong nondelegation tests when confronting capacious delegations elsewhere. And in all of this, we hope to lay the groundwork for revitalizing the separation of powers and bolstering the right to earn a living.

I. THE FOUR BROTHERS

The landmark case *Schechter Poultry* shows how to promote economic liberty through nondelegation.[3]

The Schechters, four blue-collar brothers who ran a slaughterhouse in Brooklyn, challenged the National Industrial Recovery Act (NIRA) on nondelegation grounds. NIRA authorized the President to approve "codes of fair competition."[4] Industries would draft a proposed code and the President would approve them at his discretion, subject to findings that the code would not promote monopoly and so on.[5] The President could then amend the proposal as he "in his discretion deems necessary" to serve the Act's

---

2. *See* THE FEDERALIST NO. 10 (James Madison).

3. A.L.A. Schechter Poultry Corp. v. United States, 295 U.S. 495 (1935).

4. *Id.* at 522–23.

5. *Id.*

purposes.[6] If the given industry did not propose a code, the President could create his own.[7]

To NIRA's architects, delegation was a defining and desirable feature. They wanted industry to take the lead on policymaking. NIRA's first administrator hailed it as "the charter of a new industrial self-government."[8] NIRA's drafters believed the administration should defer to businessmen's superior knowledge and their "paternalistic and fair-minded interest in the welfare of their workers."[9]

What NIRA's peddlers praised, its critics castigated. A leading critic complained that the law did not define "fair competition" and the codes could include anything "which industry agrees upon and can get approved."[10] Big business could conspire to "regulate the regulators," cloaked in foggy statutory language.[11] Thus "NIRA helped big business at a cost to smaller business."[12] As one historian put it, "Congress, in effect, had refused to formulate a definite economic policy or to decide in favor of specific economic groups. It had simply written an enabling act, an economic charter, and had then passed the buck to the Administration."[13] As we will see, many states' anti-competitive laws today follow this same pattern.

The clash between four Jewish boys from Poland and the most powerful men in the country opened with NIRA approval of the Live Poultry Code for New York City. The Code itself was a comprehensive piece of legislation, with its own administrative substrata, such as an advisory committee handpicked by industry members, and it regulated everything from prices to wages to working conditions.[14] The Code's creators had openly anti-competitive motives—they thought their code would "help" small businesses by "eliminating competition."[15]

---

6. *Id.*

7. *Id.*

8. ELLIS W. HAWLEY, THE NEW DEAL AND THE PROBLEM OF MONOPOLY 19 (1966).

9. *Id.* at 38.

10. *Id.* at 20.

11. *Id.* at 30.

12. AMITY SHLAES, THE FORGOTTEN MAN 227 (2007).

13. HAWLEY, *supra* note 8 at 33.

14. *Id.*

15. SHLAES, *supra* note 12 at 217.

New Deal attorneys targeted the Schechter brothers for NIRA's test run. The Schechters had a glimpse of what was coming when an abusive code inspector shouted at one of their customers, "I am the Code Authority, and I got a right to do anything I want, and if you don't like it, get out."[16] The inspector was not wrong. Soon after, the feds pummeled the Schechters with 60 criminal counts under the code.[17] Among these was the charge that the Schechters had violated a ban on selective killing—letting customers pick their chickens—which the Schechters observed as a religious practice.[18]

The Schechters had no input in drafting the code that ruined them. When their case reached the Supreme Court, the Schechters' attorney told the justices, "My client never assented to this code, and he was put out of business by this code."[19] These were men of low social status: Jewish Polish immigrants with bad English in an era awash with anti-Polish and antisemitic sentiment, and a small blue-collar family business. "These were not board members, not stock market players, but rather slaughterhouse men who served a market as humble as they were."[20] In other words, they were just like the many disadvantaged people without political clout who are so often the victims of crony schemes today.[21]

Yet these four blue-collar outcasts felled the New Deal. Their attorney said that the case proved that "the humblest individual receives the utmost protection under our form of government."[22] They defeated this burden on economic liberty with a simple claim: Congress cannot hand off lawmaking authority to the executive branch. The Supreme Court agreed, holding that "Congress cannot delegate legislative power to the President to exercise an unfettered discretion to make whatever laws he thinks may be needed or advisable."[23]

---

16. *Id.* at 219.

17. United States v. Schechter, 8 F. Supp. 136, 140–41 (E.D.N.Y. 1934).

18. SHLAES, *supra* note 12 at 216.

19. *Id.* at 240.

20. *Id.* at 214–15.

21. *Id.* at 214.

22. *Id.* at 244.

23. *Schechter Poultry*, 295 U.S. at 537.

These four brothers protected their right to earn a living with the nondelegation doctrine. Plaintiffs defending their right to earn a living today could learn from their success. That requires some understanding of the doctrine they used to such great effect.

II. THE DOCTRINE

The legislature cannot delegate its lawmaking authority.

This principle has its textual roots in the Constitution's vesting clauses and due process clauses. Article I, Section 1, says, "All legislative power herein granted shall be vested in a Congress of the United States." This vesting clause implies that the legislature cannot vest this power in other bodies.[24] Some federal caselaw has also drawn a nondelegation principle from the Constitution's due process clauses, reasoning that subjecting the public to policies crafted by a body without lawmaking authority does not accord with the due process of law.[25] As courts have done, this article relies on nondelegation cases relying on both constitutional sources.

A. The Doctrine's Development in the Federal Courts

A nondelegation problem arises when a statute is so vague that bureaucrats tasked with enforcement enjoy so much discretion in crafting the rules that administer the law that their discretion amounts to lawmaking authority. Courts have struggled to draw the line between legislation that leaves agencies to "fill up the details"[26] and legislation that transforms the enforcing agency into "a roving commission to inquire into evils and upon discovery correct them."[27]

The Supreme Court uses an "intelligible principle" test that asks whether Congress has "[laid] down by legislative act an intelligible principle to which the person or body authorized to exercise the delegated authority is required to conform."[28] That

---

24. *See* Gary Lawson, *Delegation and Original Meaning*, 88 VA. L. REV. 327, 335–43 (2002).

25. *See, e.g.*, Carter v. Carter Coal, 298 U.S. 238, 311 (1936).

26. Wayman v. Southard, 23 U.S. 1, 20 (1825).

27. *Schechter Poultry*, 295 U.S. at 551 (Cardozo, J., concurring).

28. Mistretta v. United States, 488 U.S. 361, 372 (1989).

test has done little to curb delegations. The Supreme Court has not stamped legislation as a nondelegation violation since the 1930s, leading some to pronounce the federal doctrine dead.[29] Nonetheless, the doctrine has still influenced statutory interpretation, nudging courts to adopt statutory interpretations that avoid delegation problems.[30]

The federal doctrine may soon rally. In 2019, four Justices expressed interest in revisiting the intelligible principle test,[31] with a fifth joining this chorus soon after.[32] Some circuit court judges have likewise called for the doctrine's revival.[33] This renewed interest has sparked much scholarship regarding the doctrine's awakening.[34] The time is ripe to consider what such a revival might mean for nondelegation claims to promote economic liberty.

B. The Doctrine's Development in the State Courts

The state courts see far more nondelegation cases than the federal courts, and they invalidate statutes on nondelegation grounds more often. Recent scholarship indicates that state courts have a much higher invalidation rate on nondelegation claims than federal courts—from 16 to 19 percent, compared to 3 percent.[35]

---

29. *See* Cass R. Sunstein & Adrian Vermeule, *Libertarian Administrative Law*, 82 U. CHI. L. REV. 393, 419 (2015).

30. *See, e.g.*, Indus. Union Dep't, AFL-CIO v. Am. Petroleum Inst., 448 U.S. 607, 645–46 (1980) (plurality opinion) ("[I]t is unreasonable to assume that Congress intended to give the Secretary the unprecedented power over American industry that would result from the Government's view. . . . A construction of the statute that avoids this kind of open-ended grant should certainly be favored.").

31. *See* Gundy v. United States, 139 S. Ct. 2116, 2130–48 (2019).

32. *See* Paul v. United States, 140 S. Ct. 342 (Mem) (2019) (Kavanaugh, J., statement respecting the denial of certiorari).

33. *See, e.g.*, Tiger Lily, LLC v. United States Dep't of Housing and Urban Development, 5 F.4th 666, 674 (6th Cir. 2021) (Thapar, J., concurring).

34. *See* Joseph Postell & Randolph J. May, *The Myth of the State Nondelegation Doctrines*, 74 ADMIN. L. REV. 263, 264 (2022); Benjamin Silver, *Nondelegation in the States*, 75 VAND. L. REV. 1211, 1212 (2022).

35. Jason Iuliano & Keith E. Whittington, *The Nondelegation Doctrine: Alive and Well*, 93 NOTRE DAME L. REV. 619, 635–36 (2017) (finding a 16% invalidation rate); Daniel Walters, *Decoding Nondelegation after Gundy: What the Experience in State Courts Tells Us about What to Expect When We're Expecting*, 71 EMORY L. J. 417, 468–69 (finding a 19% invalidation rate).

States vary in the relative strength and description of their nondelegation tests.[36] There seems, however, to be little correlation between differences in how states formulate the nondelegation test and how likely courts are to invalidate statutes on nondelegation grounds.[37] The invalidation rate is higher than the federal counterpart, whatever the test, whether it be the intelligible principle approach or something that looks stricter on paper.[38]

We will not describe state approaches in great depth here. Broadly, the tests are variations on a theme about vague lawmaking that places too much discretion in the hands of the executive. For example, Florida—which has rejected the federal test[39]—distinguishes between "flexibility in administration" and "reposing in an administrative body the power to establish fundamental policy."[40] Any tasks delegated to agencies "must be pursuant to some minimal standards and guidelines ascertainable by reference to the enactment establishing the program."[41] And Kentucky, which claims that its nondelegation doctrine is "unsurpassed" in strength,[42] merges its nondelegation test with its void for vagueness doctrine, which asks whether the legislature "has expressed its intent intelligibly, or in language that the people upon whom it is designed to operate or whom it affects can understand, or from which the courts can deduce the legislative will."[43]

Many of these tests are different ways of saying the same thing. Thus, an understanding of the varying approaches of the states requires careful synthesis of the caselaw. While we do not attempt such a comprehensive review here, we will discuss three state tests in greater depth when we examine a few case studies below.[44]

---

36. *See* Walters, *supra* note 35 at 447.

37. *Id.* at 454.

38. *Id.* at 476.

39. B.H. v. State, 645 So. 2d 987, 992 (Fla. 1994).

40. Askew v. Cross Key Waterways, 372 So. 2d 913, 924 (Fla. 1978).

41. *Id.* at 925.

42. Bd. of Trustees of Judicial Form Retirement Sys. v. Attorney General of Com. of Ky., 132 S.W.3d 770, 782 (Ky. 2003).

43. *Id.* at 779, 783.

44. *See infra* Part IV.A, B.

III. CRONIES LOVE DELEGATION

Legislatures often delegate to benefit organized, rent-seeking industries.[45] Lawmaking then trickles down to regulators who are more prone to favor incumbent industries than the legislature. This problem is evident with anti-competitive laws burdening the right to earn a living.

Delegation can "exacerbate the disproportionate influence of concentrated interests."[46] Through delegation, legislators can serve special interests without suffering the blowback from transparent favoritism. "Delegation lets legislators change their roles from actors who make hard choices on the record in dramatic confrontations to service providers who do favors for individual constituents in private, where they can take whatever stance happens to please that constituent."[47] Delegation offers legislators a tool for feeding special interests scraps under the table.

Special interests such as industry incumbents often have greater influence over agencies than they do over the legislature. "Agency heads are usually not apolitical and, indeed, concentrated interests often prevail more easily in an agency than they can in Congress."[48] When agencies call the shots, special interests do not need to lobby as many decisionmakers. Political economists have shown that special interests have greater influence when legislatures are small.[49] Lobbying pressure costs more and matters less when legislatures are large, thus reducing the strength of special interest control.[50]

This same insight applies to agencies. Smaller legislatures are more subject to special interest capture because there are fewer hands to shake, phone calls to make, and coffers to line. This is even more true of agencies. Whereas legislatures are a body of decisionmakers with diverse interests and motives that must achieve consensus, agencies are more monolithic in their interests and require fewer minds to persuade—sometimes

---

45. *See* JOHN HART ELY, DEMOCRACY & DISTRUST 132 (1980).

46. DAVID SCHOENBROD, POWER WITHOUT RESPONSIBILITY: HOW CONGRESS ABUSES THE PEOPLE THROUGH DELEGATION 125 (1993).

47. *Id.* at 104.

48. *Id.* at 13.

49. *See, e.g.*, Robert E. McCormick & Robert D. Tollison, *Wealth Transfers in a Representative Democracy, in* TOWARD A THEORY OF A RENT-SEEKING SOCIETY 293 (James M. Buchanan, Robert D. Tollison, & Gordon Tullock eds., 1980); George J. Stigler, *The Sizes of Legislatures*, 5 J. LEGAL STUD. 17 (1976).

50. *See* McCormick & Tollison, *supra* note 49 at 311.

just one. Even worse, as detailed below, agency leaders often *are* the industry they regulate, as state laws often require that licensed professionals sit on their own licensing boards.

David Schoenbrod, in his groundbreaking book on nondelegation *Power without Responsibility*,[51] used federal regulation of navel oranges to demonstrate how delegation facilitates cronyism. The New Deal's Agricultural Adjustment Act (AAA) requires the Department of Agriculture to make marketing orders that cap supply. The statute provides no guidance other than requiring that the orders make the market "orderly."[52] The department is neither an impartial nor an enlightened lawmaker. For decades, the citrus cooperative Sunkist has exerted almost total control over the navel orange market in California and Arizona thanks to the department's favoritism, made possible through broad delegations under the AAA.[53]

The department marketing order creates a growers' committee that advises the secretary, and Sunkist nominates almost half of the committee.[54] Sunkist enjoys a direct phone line to the committee, and committee staff is covered by the Sunkist pension plan.[55] Unsurprisingly, the department's control over the navel orange market favors Sunkist and disfavors unaffiliated and less powerful farmers.[56] When some regulators questioned the blatant partiality of the marketing orders, Sunkist leaned on allies in Congress, who then could—thanks to the delegated authority to the department—favor Sunkist through the dim corridors of pressuring the agency rather than in the open daylight of lawmaking.[57] Scholars have called the navel orange marketing order a "textbook illustration" of regulatory capture, made possible through the broad delegation in the

---

51. SCHOENBROD, *supra* note 46.

52. *Id.* at 4, 49.

53. *Id.* at 50–57.

54. *Id.* at 50.

55. GEORGE WILL, THE CONSERVATIVE SENSIBILITY 126 (2019).

56. SCHOENBROD, *supra* note 46 at 5–6.

57. *See id.* at 9 ("With delegation, the elected lawmakers who receive contributions from Sunkist work actively on its behalf, but they do so behind the scenes . . . rather than by casting votes on the floor of Congress or by signing bills. So they still make law, but not in the publicly accountable way that the Constitution contemplated.").

AAA.[58] As discussed below, the capture of licensing boards in the states thanks to broad delegations is even worse.

Thus, legislatures often use delegation to serve cronies who pressure or control agencies to adopt anti-competitive laws. The structural safeguards and democratic accountability imposed on the lawmaking process could check this cronyism, but legislatures escape these restraints by delegating the lawmaking function to agencies, which are freer to cater to special interests. Those concerned about regulatory capture often focus on the cozy relationship between regulator and business. We should also emphasize the arrangement that makes that relationship possible—a metacapture that occurs when a legislature favors special interests through broad delegation of lawmaking to agencies. As a commentator once said of Dodd-Frank, sometimes a law is "less important for what it explicitly [does] than for what it direct[s] others to do."[59]

IV. WHY CRONYISM IS VULNERABLE TO NONDELEGATION

Since delegation is a powerful force for cronyism, nondelegation claims are a natural rejoinder for fighting burdens on economic liberty. And a nondelegation win can have a more sweeping effect than a claim that a specific rule violates substantive due process. Perhaps the Schechter brothers could have won a narrower claim that the straight-killing rule was arbitrary. But putting an end to the delegation of lawmaking authority that allowed the arbitrary regulations in the first place was a bigger win. It was the difference between ending one anti-competitive rule in a single industry in one jurisdiction and bringing down the New Deal regime in one shot. Nondelegation claims can give plaintiffs a tool to not only prune the branches of overreaching regulators but also uproot the corrupted tree of agency lawmaking that enables the overreach.

Anti-competitive laws have two features that make them unusually vulnerable to nondelegation claims. First, they are often vague, which will be discussed further in Part V. Second, these laws are often administered by captured agencies controlled by the industries they regulate. We explain here why this second feature should heighten the level of scrutiny applied in nondelegation claims.

58. *Id.* at 56.

59. WILL, *supra* note 55 at 126.

The degree of scrutiny courts apply to a delegation should vary based on the identity of the delegatee and the institutional incentives and personal motives that influence the delegatee's exercise of delegated power. This was true with the Schechter brothers—the fact that the regulated industry was tasked with drafting the codes under NIRA concerned the Court, even if those codes were subject to presidential approval.[60]

Nondelegation challenges are more likely to succeed where there is a heightened risk of the delegatee catering to private rather than public interests. Protectionist statutes often delegate to boards and similar bodies packed with industry participants motivated to favor their own interests. This unholy amalgam of regulator and regulated will make protectionist laws more susceptible to nondelegation challenges.

A. Lessons from Private Nondelegation

The clearest example of courts' concern over the identity of the delegatee is so-called private delegation. This specialized subcategory of nondelegation has important implications for delegations to boards and other bodies that, while not private entities, nonetheless face strong incentives to favor special interests.

The landmark federal case regarding private nondelegation is *Carter v. Carter Coal Co.*[61] There, the Bituminous Coal Conservation Act delegated the power to fix maximum work hours and minimum wages of all coal miners to the mines with highest production and employment.[62] Thus, a majority of mining operations could "regulate the affairs of an unwilling minority."[63] The Court declared this law "delegation in its most obnoxious form" because it did not delegate authority to a "presumptively disinterested" public body, "but to private persons whose interests may be and often are adverse to the interests of others in the same business."[64] The Court could not abide a scheme where the delegatee is "intrusted with the power to regulate the business of another, and especially of a competitor."[65]

---

60. *See infra* notes 72–74 and accompanying text.

61. 298 U.S. 238 (1936).

62. *Id.* at 310.

63. *Id.* at 311.

64. *Id.*

65. *Id.*

Some years earlier, the Supreme Court had decided a similar issue under the due process guarantee in *State of Washington v. Roberge*.[66] There, a zoning law forbade nursing homes or orphanages in a residential district without the consent of at least two-thirds of nearby property owners.[67] The Court held such a delegation of power to the surrounding neighbors to be "repugnant to the due process clause" because neighbors were "not bound by any official duty, but are free to withhold consent for selfish reasons or arbitrarily and may subject the [plaintiff] to their will or caprice."[68] Both *Roberge* and *Carter* objected to private delegatees because the incentives and motives of the delegatee matter when considering whether a delegation is constitutional.

The state courts have likewise applied a stricter nondelegation test against delegations to private bodies.[69] Texas courts, for instance, "subject private delegations to a more searching scrutiny than their public counterparts."[70] Notably, private nondelegation claims have arisen with some frequency in the occupational licensing context, with some success.[71]

B. Extending the Private Nondelegation Principle in the Public Context

The heightened scrutiny toward private nondelegation should apply to delegations to public bodies as well if the statute's design creates undue risk that the public body will exercise its discretion to favor private interests. Consider, for example, how the Supreme Court distinguished *Schechter Poultry* when it upheld the Emergency Price Control Act against a nondelegation challenge in *Yakus v. United States*.[72] In *Yakus*, the Court confronted a nondelegation claim against the Office of Price Administration's authority to

66. 278 U.S. 116 (1928).

67. *Id.* at 118.

68. *Id.* at 122.

69. *See* Silver, *supra* note 34 at 1246.

70. Texas Boll Weevil Eradication Foundation, Inc. v. Lewellen, 952 S.W.2d 454, 469 (Tex. 1997).

71. *See, e.g.*, Ghumbir v. Kansas State Bd. of Pharmacy, 228 Kan. 579 (Kan. 1980) (Kansas law violated nondelegation doctrine by restricting pharmacy licenses only to pharmacists who graduated from a school accredited by a nongovernment association); State Bd. of Chiropractic Examiners v. Life Fellowship of Pa., 272 A.2d 478, 481 (Pa. 1971) (holding that delegation of continuing education requirements to a private chiropractic association violated nondelegation doctrine).

72. Yakus v. United States, 321 U.S. 414 (1944).

impose price controls on commodities as the administrator deemed "fair and equitable."[73] The Court upheld the statute, distinguishing *Schechter Poultry* in part because NIRA, unlike the Emergency Price Control Act, delegated the "function of formulating codes . . . not to a public official responsible to Congress or the Executive, but to private individuals engaged in the industries to be regulated."[74] Under NIRA, the President approved and amended the codes, but the industry's statutory role in the process tainted the delegation with too much private influence. Even if the executive pilots the ship, courts will apply heightened scrutiny when special interests sit as copilot.

The D.C. Circuit Court of Appeals built on this insight by applying *Carter v. Carter Coal* to a nondelegation claim against a public entity. In *Association of American Railroads v. United States Department of Transportation*,[75] the D.C. Circuit wrestled with whether Amtrak, a for-profit corporation created by statute and authorized to regulate its own competitors, was an unlawful delegation: "Does it violate due process for an entity to make law when, economically speaking, it has skin in the game?"[76] According to the court, Amtrak is a public entity, but *Carter* still applied because *Carter* was about "the self-interested character of the delegatees," not just whether the delegatee was labeled "public" or "private."[77] While a public entity is "presumptively disinterested," the stern approach taken in *Carter* will still apply if that presumption is rebutted.[78] Thus, "an economically self-interested actor," whether public or private, cannot "exercise regulatory authority over its rivals."[79]

These combined insights from *Yakus*, *Schechter Poultry*, and the Amtrak case show that courts view delegations with particular skepticism if either (a) the delegatee is closely intertwined with the special interests regulated by the delegatee or (b) the delegatee itself has a direct economic interest in the regulatory regime it oversees.

73. *Id.* at 420.

74. *Id.* at 424.

75. 821 F.3d 19 (D.C. Cir. 2016).

76. *Id.* at 23.

77. *Id.* at 28.

78. *Id.*

79. *Id.* at 27, 31. *See* Packer v. Bd. of Behavioral Science Examiners, 52 Cal. App. 3d 190, 197 (Cal. App. 1975) (rejecting nondelegation challenge to counseling licensure scheme because plaintiff had not shown "danger of control of the profession by insiders" and delegatee had "no stake in the selection of marriage, family, and child counselors").

I. Lessons from antitrust immunity

This stricter nondelegation approach where a public board or agency is too prone to special interest control finds further support in recent antitrust precedent. In *North Carolina State Board of Dental Examiners*, the Supreme Court addressed whether a dental board filled with licensed dentists enjoyed immunity from antitrust liability as a sovereign actor.[80] The Court held that antitrust liability would still apply where a state engaged in "unsupervised delegations to active market participants."[81] The Court acknowledged that "[e]ntities purporting to act under state authority might diverge from the State's considered definition of the public good. The resulting asymmetry between a state policy and its implementation can invite private self-dealing."[82]

North Carolina Dental echoed a basic tenet of nondelegation, that legislative bodies "are electorally accountable and lack the kind of private incentives characteristic of active participants in the market."[83] Importantly, the Court also rejected "formal designation" of a body as public or private, instead focusing "on the risk that active market participants will pursue private interests in restraining trade."[84] In fact, "agencies controlled by market participants are more similar to private trade associations vested by States with regulatory authority" than to a government actor.[85] What is true for antitrust is true for nondelegation.[86] Thus, under *Carter, Schechter Poultry, Yakus, American Railroad Association*, and *North Carolina Dental*, courts assessing nondelegation claims against protectionist laws should apply heightened scrutiny where the enforcing agency is vulnerable to special interest influence. And under *North Carolina Dental*, such a risk exists where occupational licensing boards are controlled by industry participants.

---

80. North Carolina Bd. of Dental Examiners v. F.T.C., 574 U.S. 494 (2015).

81. *Id.* at 506.

82. *Id.* at 507.

83. *Id.* at 508.

84. *Id.* at 510.

85. *Id.* at 511.

86. *See Texas Boll Weevil Eradication Foundation, Inc.*, 952 S.W.2d at 494 (Cornyn, J., concurring in part and dissenting in part) (arguing that courts should avoid "strained and artificial distinctions between public and private actors" when assessing nondelegation claims).

C. The Increased Scrutiny for Impure Motives Applies to Many Protectionist Laws

This principle can empower nondelegation claims brought against protectionist legislation, which often places broad discretion in the hands of bodies that are not "presumptively disinterested." This should heighten the scrutiny courts apply to nondelegation
challenges against laws burdening the right to earn a living.

Statutes often grant occupational licensing boards wide leeway to control their respec-
tive professions while filling the boards with industry incumbents with "skin in the
game" who regulate their competitors. A recent survey found that 85 percent of licensing boards are required by statute to be filled mostly by licensed industry professionals.[87]
A look at the makeup of these boards should shatter any "impression that occupational
regulation is governmental, which is to say that it is in any measure public or public-
regarding. The dirty secret behind occupational licensing boards is that very little of
what they do resembles government activity."[88]

Boards also limit what role nonindustry members play. According to Allensworth, the
laypersons or public servants who "serve" on these boards often have no influence, thanks
to problems like "rules that nonprofessional board members cannot vote, to chronic vacancies and absences of nonprofessional board members."[89] The Sunkist tale of industry control of the marketing order advisory committee that Professor Schoenbrod used
as his prime example of how delegation facilitates capture is tame compared to the board
capture rampant in almost every licensed industry. At least in the Sunkist story the committee was advisory—most state boards enjoy binding authority.

In short, industries subjected to licensing are "almost entirely self-regulating."[90] Iron-
ically, this accusation of self-regulation was the New Dealers' intent with NIRA, and it
was this strategy of industry self-regulation that *Schechter Poultry* and *Yakus* denounced
as unconstitutional delegation. Yet, once again, the situation with most state licensing

87. Rebecca Haw Allensworth, *Foxes at the Henhouse: Occupational Licensing Boards Up Close*, 105 CALIF. L. REV. 1567, 1570 (2017). *See also* Stephen Slivinski, *Choosing the Gatekeepers: How Special Interests Control Licensing Board Nominations*, Pacific Legal Foundation (2022).

88. *Id.*

89. *Id.*

90. *Id.*

boards is worse. It was bad enough in *Schechter Poultry* that private industry drafted codes for the president's approval because it risked private interests overwhelming public purpose. Here, the industry is the entity that does both the drafting and the approving. This pattern of placing special interests in charge of regulating their competitors is precisely what *Carter* called "delegation in its most obnoxious form."[91]

V. A FEW TEST RUNS

This section will test nondelegation claims against some mine-run protectionist statutes in two states with robust nondelegation doctrines and one state with a more permissive test. We hope to demonstrate that others can replicate the Schechter brothers' success in protecting the right to earn a living through nondelegation in states with strong nondelegation doctrines or otherwise.

A. Michigan, Haircuts, and Morals

Michigan is a useful test case because it is about average among states in terms of occupational licensure,[92] and scholars have marked it as a state with a "strong" nondelegation doctrine.[93] This section analyzes how Michigan's approach might apply to barbers.

1. Michigan's nondelegation doctrine

Michigan earned its place among states with a "strong" nondelegation doctrine recently[94] in *Midwest Institute of Health v. Michigan*,[95] which arose from COVID-19 emergency measures adopted under the Emergency Powers of the Governor Act.[96]

---

91. *Carter*, 298 U.S. at 311.

92. Lisa Knepper, et al., License to Work: A National Study of Burdens from Occupational Licensing 106 (3d ed. 2022); Jarrett Skorup, This Isn't Working: How Michigan's Licensing Laws Hurt Workers and Consumers 10 (2017).

93. Postell & May, *supra* note 34 at 295.

94. *Id.*

95. *In re* Certified Questions from the United States District Court, Midwest Institute of Health, PLLC v. Michigan, 958 N.W.2d 1 (Mich. 2020).

96. *Id.* at 6.

Midwest Institute of Health purported to apply the intelligible principle test,[97] though Michigan takes a more robust view of that test than the federal courts. The Act authorized the governor to declare a state of emergency upon a finding of a public crisis.[98] During the declared emergency, the governor could "promulgate reasonable orders, rules, and regulations as he or she considers necessary to protect life and property or to bring the emergency situation within the affected area under control."[99] The governor had exercised this power to close businesses, mandate masks, and take other measures familiar to all pandemic survivors.[100]

The state supreme court held the Act "constitutes an unlawful delegation of legislative power" because generic terms such as "reasonable" or "necessary" did not constrain discretion.[101] This holding departs from the federal intelligible principle test, as similar phrases have been upheld by the U.S. Supreme Court under less dire circumstances.[102] The Michigan Supreme Court's holding also stands out relative to other states, which rejected nondelegation claims against similar COVID-19 measures.[103]

The Michigan court highlighted several principles that animated its analysis. First, as a practical matter, is the statute as specific as it reasonably can be under the circumstances?[104] This sounds akin to a narrow tailoring principle, a demand that the legislature be as precise as the subject matter allows.

---

97. *Id.* at 18.

98. Mich. Compiled Laws 10.31(1).

99. *Id.*

100. *Midwest Institute of Health*, 958 N.W.2d at 20.

101. *Id.* at 22–23.

102. *See, e.g.*, Whitman v. American Trucking Ass'ns, Inc., 531 U.S. 457 (2001) (upholding ambient air quality standards to be set by EPA as "requisite to protect the public health"); New York Cent. Securities Corporation v. United States, 287 U.S. 12 (1932) (upholding law authorizing the Interstate Commerce Commission to adopt orders forcing railroad acquisitions as the commission found "just and reasonable" and "in the public interest").

103. *See* Luke Wake, *Taking Non-Delegation Doctrine Seriously*, 15 N.Y.U. J. OF LAW & LIBERTY 751, 775–76 (2022).

104. *Midwest Institute of Health*, 958 N.W.2d at 18–19.

Second, the degree of discretion allowed will narrow as the scope of the delegation expands.[105] In this case, the court was less tolerant of loose discretion because the Act granted the governor power over the entire economy.[106]

Third, the constitutionality of delegated authority depends on how long the authority lasts.[107] Here, despite the delegated authority hinging on the presence of a temporary emergency, it had an indefinite duration.[108]

Finally, the Court expressed concern with this vast authority's "concentration in a single individual."[109] While the Court did not draw a broader principle from this concern, it appears from context that the Court recognized that the identity of the delegatee matters. Nondelegation should consider the risk that the delegatee will exercise lawmaking authority to pursue interests contrary to the public's.

These are not new ideas. The Supreme Court itself has mouthed some of them in dicta. It is the Michigan court's commitment to taking these ideas seriously that makes it a friendly arena for litigating nondelegation claims.

2. Delegation of licensing to the Board of Barber Examiners

Michigan delegates broad discretion to self-interested licensing boards and requires licenses for about 160 occupations.[110] It is one of the worst states for board capture, where 100 percent of licensing boards are dominated by licensed professionals.[111] For instance, statute requires that six members of the Board of Barber Examiners must be licensed barbers.[112] There is no statutory minimum on board size.[113] Currently, the board has nine

---

105. *Id. See also* Stephen Markman, *Remarks on In re Certified Questions*, 15 N.Y.U. J. OF LAW & LIBERTY 587, 594–96 (2022).

106. *Id.* at 19.

107. *Id.* at 19–20.

108. *Id.*

109. *Id.* at 31.

110. SKORUP, *supra* note 92 at 1.

111. Allensworth, *supra* note 87 at 1609.

112. MCL 339.1102.

113. *Id.*

members.[114] Even assuming that some of these members are not barbers, the current board size ensures industry dominance.

The statute grants the Board of Barber Examiners open discretion on various vague standards. For example, a license applicant must be of "good moral character."[115] A license applicant must also pass an examination "approved by the board."[116] A holder of a license from another state can get a license so long as the requirements for licensure in the other state are "substantially equivalent" to Michigan's own requirements "as determined by the department."[117] A license to run a barbershop, moreover, is subject to whatever sanitation standards the board sets.[118] No explicit standards guide the board's exercise of discretion on any of these matters.

We will only examine a few of these. The "good moral character" standard is common across all Michigan's licensing regimes and those in other states.[119] Statute defines this phrase as "the propensity on the part of an individual to serve the public in the licensed area in a fair, honest, and open manner."[120] Critics have complained that the "good moral character" standard in general is vague and offers too much discretion to boards,[121] who routinely abuse the standard to shut out specific groups like ex-offenders.[122] The Board of Barber Examiners appears to have adopted no specific regulations regarding the "good moral character" standard, leaving itself with wide discretion to apply the standard how it wishes on a case-by-case basis.

The statute also leaves examination standards up to the board, with no language describing how the board should exercise this discretion. The board is free to decide the

---

114. *See* Board of Barber Examiners, *available at* https://somgovweb.state.mi.us/BoardCrmWeb /boarddetail/b3afbef9-fab9-ed11-83fe-001dd804fc82.

115. MCL 339.1108(1)(b).

116. *Id.* at 1108(1)(d).

117. *Id.* at 1108(2).

118. *Id.* at 1111, 1112.

119. SKORUP, *supra* note 92 at 12–13; Nick Sibilla, *Barred from Working: A Nationwide Study of Occupational Licensing Barriers for Ex-Offenders*, Institute for Justice (2020).

120. MCL 338.41(1).

121. Larry Craddock, *"Good Moral Character" as a Licensing Standard*, 28 J. NAT'L ASS'N ADMIN. L. JUDICIARY 449, 451–52 (2008).

122. Sibilla, *supra* note 119 at 2–6.

length of the test, its rigor, subject matters covered, passing scores, and so on. The board has exercised this discretion to require all applicants to pass an exam created and administered by a private company, PSI Services, LLC.[123] Hence, a board controlled by industry professionals has subdelegated the testing for all barber licenses to a private entity.[124]

3. Do barbers exercise lawmaking authority?

Can aspiring barbers follow the Schechter brothers? We think so.

As a threshold matter, heightened scrutiny should apply here. As both Michigan's and the federal doctrine require, courts should demand more specific statutory guidelines where there is a risk that the delegatee is likely to pursue private interests. Here, board members overseeing barbers are mostly if not all barbers themselves. Thus, the board has been "intrusted with the power to regulate the business . . . of a competitor."[125]

The scope of delegated authority, a key element in Michigan's nondelegation analysis, likely cuts against the statute. Unlike *Schechter Poultry* and *Midwest Institute of Health*, the Board does not exercise authority over the entire economy. Yet power over a whole industry is not a "narrow subject." After all, the unlawful delegations in *Carter* and *Association of American Railroads* each involved regulatory control within a single industry, and the delegation in *Roberge* involved piecemeal property approvals. Likewise, *Panama Refining Co. v. Ryan*, decided just months before *Schechter Poultry*, involved a yet narrower authority over petroleum transportation.[126] Broad control over an entire industry should demand specific statutory standards. Duration of the delegation of course would favor a plaintiff, as the licensing authority is a permanent investiture of authority in the board.

The "good moral character" standard is vulnerable to challenge. Even with the definition—"the propensity on the part of an individual to serve the public in the licensed area in a fair, honest, and open manner"—the standard is subjective, such that an agency

123. Mich. Admin. R. 339.6021(2).

124. *See State Bd. of Chiropractic Examiners*, 272 A.2d at 481 (holding that delegation of continuing education requirements to a private chiropractic association violated nondelegation doctrine).

125. *Carter*, 298 U.S. at 311.

126. Panama Refining Co. v. Ryan, 293 U.S. 388 (1935).

enforcing it without further guidance cannot help but make policy judgments. Under *Midwest Institute of Health*, we ask whether the legislature was as specific as we could reasonably expect given the complexities of the subject matter. Here, it surely could have been more precise. Good morals do not demand complicated scientific expertise or other specialized knowledge. In fact, the statute itself demonstrates the legislature's capacity to define moral ideas with specificity by listing "prohibited conduct" that can result in license suspension, such as engaging in "fraud, deceit, or dishonesty in practicing an occupation."[127] If nothing else, nondelegation could influence a court to interpret the moral character standard narrowly to avoid constitutional peril.

Delegating something like standards for examination might be a closer question. The statute offers no guidance here, simply stating that a license requires that the applicant "[p]asses an examination approved by the board and the department."[128] Taken literally, the board could require barbers to pass an examination cataloguing every animal species in the Amazon and still operate within the statute's confines. It should cause particular concern that a body with an incentive to limit entry to the profession is free to make the exam as difficult or arbitrary as possible. It is doubly troubling that the board is free to subdelegate this authority to a wholly private body, as it has done here.

Courts may see this as a topic where the legislature cannot reasonably be more specific, given that a generalist lawmaker does not know what a barber must know, and can therefore let the agency "fill up the details." The legislature can, however, outline the subject matter to be covered, such as hygiene, sanitation, or hairstyles, and it can offer some guidelines to govern matters like test length, passing scores, and so on. A court might consider such standards as implied given the subject matter. *Midwest Institute of Health*, however, was not willing to tolerate implied guidance. Though a tougher question, if *Midwest Health* is taken seriously, as well as the captured nature of the board, then the exam standard is likely an unlawful delegation. At minimum, a nondelegation argument could press the court to interpret the statute in a manner that limits the board's discretion.

127. MCL 339.605(b).
128. MCL 339.1108(1)(d).

B. Montana, Garbage, and Public Necessity

Montana is also categorized as a "strong" nondelegation state[129] and "may be the state with the largest number of statutes invalidated on nondelegation grounds in recent decades."[130] In testing Montana's approach, we did not select a specific occupational licensing regime because we want to highlight a common protectionist barrier across the states: certificate-of-need laws.

1. Montana's nondelegation doctrine

Unlike Michigan, Montana has expressly rejected the intelligible principle test. The state supreme court has noted "that the trend is away from requiring that statutory standards or guides be specified" but that even if "this may be the trend under federal law and in some states, it's not Montana's position."[131]

In Montana, delegations to agencies "must provide, with reasonable clarity, limitations upon the agency's discretion and provide the agency with policy guidance."[132] A prescribed limit on authority is too broad if "the officer or board will have unascertainable limits within which to act."[133]

Montana's emphasis on "prescribed limits" on the agency's power is noteworthy. The intelligible principle test requires that the statute outline only what the agency can do, not "clearly prescribed" *limits* on that authority.[134] Granted, an agency cannot do what a statute does not authorize it to do, but in practice, open-ended statutes focused on grants of power often let the agencies themselves define what the limits on that power might be. Montana's demand for boundaries articulated by the legislature would "not allow for an administrative board to legislate the limits of its own power."[135]

129. Walters, *supra* note 35 at 447.

130. Postell & May, *supra* note 34 at 295.

131. *Matter of Authority to Conduct Sav. and Loan Activities in the State of Mont. by Gate City Savings and Loan Association of Fargo, North Dakota*, 597 P.2d 84, 89 (Mont. 1979).

132. *In re Petition to Transfer Territory from High School Dist. No. 6 v. Lame Deer High School Dist.*, 15 P.3d 447, 450 (Mont. 2000).

133. Bacus v. Lake County, 354 P.2d 1056, 1062 (Mont. 1960).

134. White v. State, 759 P.2d 971, 977 (Mont. 1988).

135. *Id.*

The Montana Supreme Court has wielded this test with surprising rigor. For instance, in *Lame Deer High School*, the court addressed whether a law granting "authority to county superintendents of schools to grant or deny petitions to transfer territory among school districts[] is an unconstitutional delegation of legislative power."[136] The Supreme Court of Montana held the delegation unlawful despite guidance to the superintendents that was more detailed than statutes upheld by federal courts. For example, the transfer could only occur under specific conditions based on location of nearby schools, changes in the taxable value of the district, and so on.[137] After all these conditions were met, the superintendent could grant the petition, but his decision had to be "based on the effects that the transfer would have on those residing in the territory proposed for transfer as well as those residing in the remaining territory of the high school district."[138]

The court did not mind the superintendent acting in the "role of factfinder" regarding objective factors such as school proximity and taxable value.[139] But these objective criteria could not save the final "effects" factor, which was "unchecked by any standard, policy or rule of decision."[140] *Lame Deer* reflects a necessary-and-sufficient principle: specific, objective criteria cannot save a statute from nondelegation concerns if those criteria are only *necessary* to the exercise of a power, but not *sufficient* to trigger it. If the final decision, after exhausting the necessary objective criteria, still rests with the discretion of the administrator, then the delegation is unlawful. This may be an application of Montana's focus on not only specific *grants* of power but also specific *limits* on power. Despite the statute's list of objective criteria, the statute did not limit the superintendent to considering those objective criteria, leaving him instead with an open-ended "effects" factor that did not restrain his authority.

2. Certificates of need

Certificate-of-need laws appear often in the healthcare and transportation industries and require that businesses obtain permission from a state board before opening or

---

136. *Lame Deer High School*, 15 P.3d at 449.

137. *Id.*

138. *Id.* at 451.

139. *Id.*

140. *Id.*

expanding businesses. Such laws are in effect in some 35 states.[141] Often, the regulated business must demonstrate the need for its services to obtain a certificate and allow incumbent businesses to oppose applications.[142] Such laws can impose a serious burden on the right to earn a living.[143]

Montana requires garbage haulers to obtain a "certificate of public convenience and necessity" from the Public Service Commission.[144] The statute instructs the commission to "consider:" "the transportation being furnished," "the likelihood of the proposed service being permanent and continuous," and "the effect that the proposed transportation service may have on other forms of transportation service that are essential and indispensable to the communities to be affected by the proposed transportation service."[145] Finally, "a determination of public convenience and necessity may include a consideration of competition."[146]

The Public Service Commission does not suffer from direct industry dominance. The commission has five elected members, with vacancies filled by governor appointment.[147] The commission is not wholly insulated from industry involvement, however. When an application for a certificate is filed with the commission, the commission must provide notice to interested parties (incumbent businesses), who have a statutory privilege to protest an application, demand a hearing, and participate in the hearing as a party.[148]

141. Matthew D. Mitchell and Christopher Koopman, *40 Years of Certificate-of-Need Laws across America*, Mercatus Center (2016).

142. *See, e.g.*, KY. REV. STAT. 281 630(1) (requiring moving companies to obtain a certificate of public convenience and necessity by proving that "the existing transportation service is inadequate, and that the proposed service . . . is or will be required by the present or future public convenience and necessity"); LA. ADMIN. CODE TIT. 48, 12523(C)(4) ("The burden is on the applicant to provide data and evidence to effectively establish the probability of serious, adverse consequences to recipients' ability to access health care if the provider is not allowed to be licensed.").

143. *See* Anastasia Boden, *She Tried to Start a Business, but Was Told It Wasn't Needed. Supreme Court Should Change That*, USA TODAY (Sep. 19, 2023).

144. Mont. Code Ann. § 69-12-314(1).

145. *Id.* 69-12-323(2)(a).

146. *Id.* 69-12-323(2)(b).

147. *See id.* 69-1-101 et seq.

148. *Id.* 69-12-321.

Industry incumbents protest routinely when a new application is filed, and a protest significantly reduces an application's chance at success.[149]

3. Applying Montana's test

This law would likely fail Montana's nondelegation test.[150] Again, we first address the threshold question of whether heightened statutory standards are required under *Carter* because the delegatee faces undue influence.

The board here is democratically elected, with no statutory mandate that board members hold certificates or licenses related to the industries they regulate. Still, there is danger of undue industry influence through the statutory protest procedure.[151] Industry incumbents often protest new applications, which triggers a hearing requirement at which the protesting incumbent participates.[152] While the rulemakers themselves may not have a direct self-interest, this is still akin to *Schechter Poultry*, where industry incumbents had a legal right to participate in the administrative process. In *Schechter Poultry*, the industry involvement occurred at the rulemaking stage, whereas here the protesting incumbents can involve themselves at a quasi-judicial stage. In both cases, the industry lacks authority to adopt binding rules, but their influence is nonetheless real. Courts may hold, however, that since the industry incumbents are not involved in the ex ante rulemaking process, their role is too tangential to overcome the presumption that the board is operating in a disinterested manner.

There may be another avenue for demanding heightened specificity, however. Montana's constitution recognizes the right to earn a living as fundamental.[153] The U.S. Supreme Court has held that where a statute regulates a constitutionally recognized right, courts should "construe narrowly all delegated powers that curtail or dilute them."[154]

---

149. *See* Noland v. Montana, No. DV-15-2022-0001308-CR (Mont. Dist. Ct. 2023), Memorandum in Support of Plaintiff's Motion for Summary Judgment at 6.

150. *See* Postell & May, *supra* note 34 at 298 (speculating that Montana's test would endanger public-convenience-and-necessity laws).

151. *See* MCA 69-12-321.

152. *See id.* 69-12-321(2).

153. Wadsworth v. State, 275 Mont. 287, 299, 301–02 (Mont. 1996).

154. Kent v. Dulles, 357 U.S. 116, 129 (1958). *See also* Markman, *supra* note 105 at 597.

Thus, states like Montana and Texas[155] that recognize heightened protection for the right to earn a living may offer an opportunity to demand higher statutory safeguards on delegations touching on that right.

Even if a heightened standard does not apply, the public-convenience-and-necessity law is likely unlawful. In *Lame Deer*, the Montana Supreme Court held that unlawful delegation had occurred where the county superintendents could transfer territory among districts "based on *the effects* the transfer would have on those residing in the territory."[156] The motor carrier certificate statute uses similar language, directing the Public Service Commission to "consider" "*the effect* that the proposed transportation service may have on other forms of transportation service that are essential and indispensable to the communities affected by the proposed transportation service or that might be affected by that proposed transportation service."[157] The commission is not told what effects to consider or how to weigh them. This is the same "unguided judgment" disapproved in *Lame Deer*.[158]

Further, the statute only dictates what the Public Service Commission "shall consider" in the exercise of its authority. It offers no "clearly prescribed" limits on the exercise of that authority.[159] Since the statute only tells the commission what to "consider" with no guidance on how to weigh or apply those considerations, the statute grants the board authority "to legislate the limits of its own power," something Montana forbids.[160]

C. Washington, Adequate Safeguards, and Sick Animals

In our final test run, we hope to show that protectionist laws are vulnerable to nondelegation even in those states with "weak" nondelegation doctrines. This section applies Washington's permissive test to occupational licensing of the veterinary industry.

---

155. *See* Patel v. Texas Dept. of Licensing and Regulation, 469 S.W.3d 69, 86–887 (Tex. 2015).

156. *Lame Deer*, 15 P.3d at 451 (emphasis added).

157. MCA 69-12-323(2)(a)(iii) (emphasis added).

158. *Lame Deer*, 15 P.3d at 451.

159. *White*, 759 P.2d at 977.

160. *Id.*

1. Washington's nondelegation test

Scholars have categorized Washington's test as "weak."[161] It has two parts. "First, the legislature must provide standards or guidelines in general terms what is to be done and the administrative body which is to do it."[162] "Second, adequate procedural safeguards" must "exist to control arbitrary administrative action and any administrative abuse of discretionary power."[163] This "procedural safeguards" prong is common among states with a more permissive approach.[164]

The state supreme court applied this test in 2022 to a law requiring the Department of Labor and Industries to calculate prevailing wage rates based on whichever collective bargaining agreement (CBA) sets the highest wages.[165] Challengers claimed this scheme was a nondelegation violation because it left the determination of a legally binding wage rate up to self-interested private parties negotiating outside government supervision.

While acknowledging that the law did incorporate private interests into lawmaking through the bargaining process, the court nonetheless rejected the nondelegation challenge.[166] On the first prong—standards and guidelines—the court held that the law had a clear standard that asked the agency to make a factual determination of which CBA offered the highest wage rate.[167]

On the second prong—adequate procedural safeguards—the court held that the risk of the self-interest or collusion between bargaining parties infecting public policy was checked by the procedural protections in the collective bargaining process itself, which would protect the public against collusive behavior by private parties that could result in arbitrarily inflated wages for public contracts.[168]

---

161. Postell & May, *supra* note 34 at 45–46.

162. Associated General Contractors of Washington v. State, 518 P.3d 639, 644 (Wash. 2022).

163. *Id.*

164. Gary Greco, *Standards or Safeguards: A Survey of the Delegation Doctrine in the States*, 8 ADMIN. L.J. AM. U. 567, 598–99 (1994).

165. *Associated General Contractors*, 518 P.3d at 641.

166. *Id.* at 649.

167. *Id.* at 647.

168. *Id.*

2. Veterinary medicine in Washington

We test Washington's approach against the state's veterinary licensing regime, which highlights another common protectionist barrier: scope-of-practice rules.

The Washington Veterinary Board of Governors suffers from industry capture. Of the nine-member board, six must be licensed veterinarians, one must be a veterinary technician, one can be either a veterinarian or a technician, and one must be a layperson.[169] A majority constitutes a quorum, and a majority vote of a quorum can adopt rules, meaning that it's possible for a three-member bloc to approve rules binding the profession.[170]

The board's authority is broad. It "shall develop and administer, or approve, or both, a licensure examination in the subjects determined by the board to be essential to the practice of veterinary medicine."[171] This expressly includes authority to approve an examination from a private association.[172] More expansively, the board "may adopt rules necessary to carry out the purposes" of the chapter governing veterinary medicine. The statute does not offer guidelines for the exercise of this authority, only specifying that board authority "includes" the power to create "[s]tandards for the performance of the duties and responsibilities of veterinary technicians" and "[s]tandards prescribing requirements for veterinary medical facilities" and continuing education.[173]

The board has exercised its broad discretion not only to erect barriers to performing almost any work related to animal care—such as lengthy and expensive schooling at an accredited institution[174]—but also to limit the economic opportunities of veterinary technicians to compete with licensed veterinarians through scope-of-practice rules. Licensed veterinary technicians and assistants cannot, for instance, initiate treatment on their own prerogative, prescribe medicine, or diagnose illness.[175] The tasks a veterinary technician or assistant can perform often require direct veterinarian supervision.[176]

169. Wash. Rev. Code Ann. § 18.92.021 (1).

170. *Id.* 18.92.021(4).

171. *Id.* 18.92.030(1).

172. *Id.*

173. *Id.* 18.92.030(2).

174. *See* Wash. Admin. Code (WAC) 246-933-220 et seq.

175. WAC 246-935-050(1).

176. *Id.* 246-935-050(2)–(3).

Licensed professionals are known to use scope-of-practice and supervision rules to stave off lower-cost competitors.[177] The single required veterinary technician on the board lacks voting power to protect the interests of their profession against the six licensed veterinarian board members.

3. Applying Washington's test

Even under Washington's permissive test, a nondelegation challenge to the veterinary licensing scheme could have promise.

The "standards or guidelines" step only requires the statute to identify the delegatee and the "general terms" of the delegation. The state supreme court has said that a statute satisfied this first prong when it simply stated that an agency "shall issue from time to time reasonable rules and regulations" to carry out the statute's purpose.[178] If this standardless language passes muster under the first prong, a generalized delegation to the veterinary board to make rules "necessary to carry out the purposes" of the statute probably satisfies it as well.

The second prong, adequate procedural safeguards to prevent abuse of discretionary power, has more potential. Here, the risk of abuse of discretionary power is high thanks to board capture. In *Associated General Contractors*, the Washington Supreme Court held that the risk of self-interested collusion infecting the process for setting the prevailing wage was mitigated by federal laws that oversaw the collective bargaining process and promoted a genuinely arms-length agreement between workers and employers.

There is no comparable procedural safeguard here. Neither the legislature nor public officials within the state's health department oversee or supervise the rulemaking activities of the board to check self-interested board actions. Indeed, the board has engaged in such self-interested activity by restricting competitors through scope-of-practice rules. It should also matter that—unlike with the prevailing wage statute—violation of board rules can carry criminal penalties.[179] While Washington has not held that heightened

---

177. *See* Shirley V. Svorny & Michael F. Cannon, *Health Care Workforce Reform: COVID-19 Spotlights Need for Changes to Clinician Licensing*, Cato Institute Policy Analysis (2020).

178. *Barry & Barry v. State Dep't of Motor Vehicles*, 81 Wash. 2d 155, 158 (1972).

179. *See* RCW 18.130.190(7), 18.92.240.

safeguards apply where agencies enjoy the power to define criminal offenses, other states have.[180]

CONCLUSION

Legislatures have powerful incentives to use delegation to cater to industry incumbents, as do the agencies that exercise delegated power. Hence, unbounded delegations like the law defeated by the Schechter brothers are a common feature of protectionist laws.

Nondelegation claims give litigants a legal theory that meshes well with this classic tale of regulatory capture. The nondelegation lens helps litigants tell the cronyism story under the umbrella of one overarching legal theory; the arbitrariness of the regulation, the vague standards of the legislation, the self-interested nature of agency officials, and the burdens on the right to earn a living—all these facts matter to a nondelegation claim.

Not only do these claims paint a powerful narrative, but they have a genuine chance at winning. Common protectionist laws like occupational licensing and certificate-of-need laws are rife with "delegation running riot."[181] And the remedy available for a nondelegation violation is powerful—not only does it have the potential to alleviate one arbitrary burden on the right to earn a living, but it can also stop legislatures from serving special interests under the table through delegated power.

With federal judges ready to dust off the nondelegation doctrine and state courts willing to impose serious scrutiny on delegations, the time is ripe for litigants to bring nondelegation claims to promote the right to earn a living. We have role models in the Schechters, four humble brothers from the lowest social class of their era who brought down the New Deal. If they can do it, so can we.

---

180. *See, e.g.*, *B.H.*, 645 So.2d at 993.

181. *Schechter Poultry*, 295 U.S. at 553 (Cardozo, J., concurring).

Protecting Economic Liberty under Both Article IV and the Fourteenth Amendment

By Skylar Croy and Daniel P. Lennington*

INTRODUCTION

James Madison wrote that a "just government" necessarily protects economic liberty.[1] Echoing this sentiment, Thomas Jefferson explained a few years later that "a wise and frugal government . . . shall not take from the mouth of labor the bread it has earned."[2] Their emphasis on economic liberty was well supported by the common law dating back centuries.[3] In 1614, for example, English courts held that people had a right to enter certain professions without first completing an apprenticeship,[4] and about a decade later, another English court invalidated an ordinance granting a monopoly to a

* Skylar Croy is Associate Counsel and Daniel P. Lennington is Deputy Counsel at Wisconsin Institute for Law & Liberty, Inc. The authors are grateful to the Americans for Prosperity Foundation, the Goldwater Institute, the Institute for Justice, the New England Law Foundation, the Pacific Legal Foundation, and Professor Steven G. Calabresi. Each submitted excellent briefs in a recent case, which identified many of the primary sources relied upon throughout this article. These briefs can be read at https://www .supremecourt.gov/docket/docketfiles/html/public/22-1208.html. The authors are also grateful for the scholarship of Timothy Sandefur and Professors Randy E. Barnett and Evan D. Bernick.

1. James Madison, *Property* (1792), *in* JAMES MADISON: WRITINGS 515, 516 (1999).

2. Thomas Jefferson, President, First Inaugural Address (Mar. 4, 1801), FOUNDERS ONLINE, https:// founders.archives.gov/documents/Jefferson/01-33-02-0116-0004.

3. Timothy Sandefur, *The Right to Earn a Living*, 6 CHAPMAN L. REV. 207, 209 (2003).

4. The Case of the Tailors, &c. of Ipswich, 77 Eng. Rep. 1218 (K.B. 1614); *see also* Allen v. Tooley, 80 Eng. Rep. 1055 (K.B. 1614).

chimney-repair company.[5] In one of these cases, the great jurist Sir Edward Coke explained that "no man could be prohibited from working in any lawful trade, for the law abhors idleness. . . ."[6] In the eighteenth century, Sir William Blackstone explained that the common law demanded that "every man might use what trade he pleased," and a statute in degradation of this principle was "general[ly] confined."[7] In America's first hundred years, court after court protected economic liberty.[8] Modern jurists and scholars, including the Goldwater Institute's Timothy Sandefur, have chronicled the historical record at length, and their work defies any notion that economic liberty is a newfound legal concept.[9]

Against this backdrop, the lack of significant and well recognized constitutional protection for economic liberty in modern jurisprudence is surprising. Section 1 of the Fourteenth Amendment contains two clauses often cited in discussions about economic liberty—the Privileges or Immunities Clause and the Due Process Clause: "No State shall make or enforce any law which shall abridge the privileges or immunities of citizens of the United States; nor shall any State deprive any person of life, liberty, or property, without due process of law. . . ." Under the Privileges or Immunities Clause, economic liberty as a constitutional right never had much of a chance. In 1873, just five years after adoption of the Fourteenth Amendment, the U.S. Supreme Court narrowly construed the Privileges or Immunities Clause in the *Slaughter-House* decision.[10] The Court held that the clause protects only rights that are "placed under the special care of the Federal government."[11] In a decision about two decades after *Slaughter-House*, the Court indicated that one such right could be the right to "carry on interstate commerce,"[12] but the

---

5. Les Brick-Layers & Tilers v. Les Plaisterers, 81 Eng. Rep. 871, 872 (K.B. 1624).

6. Tailors of Ipswich, 77 Eng. Rep. at 1219; *see also* Colgate v. Bacheler, 78 Eng. Rep. 1097, 1097 (K.B. 1602) (explaining a person "ought not to be abridged of his trade and living").

7. 1 WILLIAM BLACKSTONE, COMMENTARIES *427–28.

8. Sandefur, *supra* note 3, at 225–27 (collecting decisions).

9. *See generally* Golden Glow Tanning Salon, Inc. v. Columbus, 52 F.4th 974, 982–84 (2022) (Ho, J., concurring); Porter v. State, 913 N.W.2d 842, 855–59 (Wis. 2018) (Rebecca Grassl Bradley & Kelly, J. J., dissenting); Sandefur, *supra* note 3.

10. Slaughter-House Cases, 83 U.S. 36 (1873).

11. *Id.* at 78.

12. Crutcher v. Kentucky, 141 U.S. 47, 57 (1891) ("To carry on interstate commerce is not a franchise or a privilege granted by the state; it is a right which every citizen of the United States is entitled to exercise under the constitution. . . .").

concept of "interstate commerce" then was much more limited than it has become, and the Court's jurisprudence on the Privileges or Immunities Clause has not kept pace.[13] Now, courts across the country routinely—and typically, without much thought—hold that "the right to earn a living in a lawful occupation of one's choice" is not protected by the clause.[14] In fact, scholars have characterized the clause as "contribut[ing] next to nothing to contemporary law."[15] Ouch. As the Fifth Circuit recently noted, the Due Process Clause was once used "aggressive[ly]" to "review . . . state regulation of business"; however, since the Progressive Era of the early 20th century, courts have generally upheld restrictions on economic liberty for merely having a rational basis,[16] as if economic liberty does not implicate fundamental rights like the right to earn a living.[17]

While the Privileges or Immunity Clause has been narrowly construed, the U.S. Supreme Court has never imposed such a cramped construction on the Privileges and Immunities Clause of Article IV, Section 2, which reads: "The Citizens of each State shall be entitled to all Privileges and Immunities of citizens in the several States." In this article, to avoid confusion, the Privileges or Immunities Clause is referred to as the "Fourteenth Amendment Clause" and the Privileges and Immunities Clause as the "Article IV Clause." Usually, similar language is given a similar construction,[18] but these two clauses, despite textual similarities, are treated quite differently.[19]

As currently construed, the Article IV Clause protects some aspects of economic liberty to a much greater degree than the Due Process Clause, making the Article IV Clause

---

13. Although it is not the focus of this article, one way to protect economic liberty might be to rely on the ever-expanding definition of "interstate commerce," which is now understood to cover just about everything even related to commerce. *See generally* Wickard v. Filburn, 317 U.S. 111 (1942).

14. Newell-Davis v. Phillips, No. 22–30166, 2023 WL 1880000, at *2, 6 (5th Cir. Feb. 10, 2023), *cert. denied*, 144 S. Ct. 98.

15. RANDY E. BARNETT & EVAN D. BERNICK, THE ORIGINAL MEANING OF THE FOURTEENTH AMENDMENT: ITS LETTER & SPIRIT 41 (2021).

16. St. Joseph Abbey v. Castille, 712 F.3d 215, 221–27 (5th Cir. 2013); *see also* David E. Bernstein, *The Due Process Right to Pursue a Lawful Occupation: A Brighter Future Ahead?*, 126 YALE L.J. FORUM 287 (2016).

17. *But see infra* Part I (explaining the right to earn a living has been considered a fundamental right in other contexts).

18. ANTONIN SCALIA & BRYAN A. GARNER, READING LAW: THE INTERPRETATION OF LEGAL TEXTS 170 (2012).

19. *Slaughter-House*, 83 U.S. at 73–79; *see also* United States v. Cruikshank, 92 U.S. (2 Otto) 542, 549 (1875).

unique. For example, in *Supreme Court of Virginia v. Friedman*, the U.S. Supreme Court stated that "the practice of law, like other occupations[,] . . . is sufficiently basic to the national economy to be deemed a privilege protected by the [c]lause."[20] In another decision, the Court explained that "the pursuit of a common calling is one of the most fundamental . . . privileges" safeguarded by the clause.[21] Problematically though, under current jurisprudence, even if a right is among those protected by the clause, the clause is irrelevant unless a state is treating its own residents better than nonresidents.[22] In other words, the Article IV Clause is relegated to preventing discrimination by states; it is not a robust protection of right in all circumstances. So, while its jurisprudence supports economic liberty, the Article IV Clause can be applied only in relatively narrow circumstances. In contrast, the rights protected by the Fourteenth Amendment Clause, while fewer, can be protected even in the absence of discrimination.

Relying on the Article IV Clause, this article proposes a litigation strategy that could be employed to persuade the U.S. Supreme Court that the Fourteenth Amendment Clause protects economic liberty. This strategy suggests working within existing doctrinal frameworks by first bringing more economic liberty cases under the Article IV Clause. Cases that involve the rights to engage in interstate commerce and travel may be ideal because these rights touch on national issues, thereby roughly fitting within the doctrinal framework laid out in *Slaughter-House* for the Fourteenth Amendment Clause.[23] After building on existing Article IV Clause jurisprudence, step 2 is to highlight textual similarities, historical sources, and precedential reasons that the Fourteenth Amendment Clause and the Article IV Clause should be construed to protect largely the same set of rights. The overlap between the rights protected by these clauses should be much more than it presently is. Under this strategy, bringing a step-2 case under the Fourteenth Amendment Clause nearly identical to a previously successful step-1 case under the Article IV Clause would force any court (and eventually the U.S. Supreme Court) to confront this fundamental question: How can a "privilege" or "immunity" clearly protected

20. Sup. Ct. of Va. v. Friedman, 487 U.S. 59, 66 (1988).

21. United Bldg. & Const. Trades Council of Camden Cnty. & Vicinity v. Mayor & Council of the City of Camden, 465 U.S. 208, 219 (1984).

22. *E.g.*, Toomer v. Witsell, 334 U.S. 385, 395–96 (1948).

23. *Slaughter-House*, 83 U.S. at 79–80.

by Article IV *not* also be a "privilege" or "immunity" protected under the Fourteenth Amendment?

Overall, the goal of this litigation strategy is to move the Supreme Court gradually toward recognizing the similarities between the two clauses, rather than calling for an immediate rejection of *Slaughter-House*, which the Court appears unwilling to do. Indeed, in 2023, the Court denied a petition for certiorari explicitly asking it to overrule *Slaughter-House*.[24] That denial does not bode well for any nonincrementalist approach, and so, this article proposes an incremental one.

I. AN OVERVIEW OF THE ARTICLE IV CLAUSE

In 1978, the U.S. Supreme Court recognized that the Article IV Clause "has been over-shadowed" by the Fourteenth Amendment Clause, which contains "similar language."[25] The Article IV Clause, the Court said, "is not one the contours of which have been precisely shaped by the process and war of constant litigation and judicial interpretation...."[26] In contrast, the Fourteenth Amendment Clause has been studied extensively, perhaps because scholars recognize its potential to resolve many perceived problems.[27] The Court questioned the relationship between the two clauses, noting their "relationship, if any," was "less than clear."[28]

Since then, scholars have dedicated significant time to documenting the original understanding of the Article IV Clause and its relation to the Fourteenth Amendment Clause.[29] The Article IV Clause, like most of Article IV, deals with interstate relations.[30] It is like a provision in the Articles of Confederation, which read:

> The better to secure and perpetuate mutual friendship and intercourse among the people of the different States in this Union, the free inhabitants of each of these States, paupers, vagabonds and fugitives from Justice excepted, shall be entitled to

---

24. *Newell-Davis*, 144 S. Ct. 98.

25. Baldwin v. Fish & Game Comm'n of Mont., 436 U.S. 371, 379 (1978).

26. *Id.*

27. *Id.* at 379–80; *see also* BARNETT & BERNICK, *supra* 15, at 41.

28. *Baldwin*, 436 U.S. at 380.

29. *E.g.*, BARNETT & BERNICK, *supra* note 15, at 54–60.

30. *Baldwin*, 436 U.S. at 379.

all privileges and immunities of free citizens in the several States; and the people of each State shall have free ingress and regress to and from any other State, and shall enjoy therein all the privileges of trade and commerce, subject to the same duties, impositions and restrictions as the inhabitants thereof respectively provided that such restrictions shall not extend so far as to prevent the removal of property imported into any State, to any other State, of which the owner is an inhabitant; provided also that no imposition, duties or restriction shall be laid by any State, on the property of the United States, or either of them.[31]

Notably, this provision explicitly protected "all the privileges of trade and commerce." The absence of such language in the Article IV Clause should not be understood as indicating it does not protect economic liberty. As an 1821 decision explained, "There was . . . objection" to the provision; specifically, it "employ[ed] the most comprehensive words" after "privileges and immunities," which potentially "weakened the force of those terms" through enumeration.[32]

The Article IV Clause was not discussed much at the Constitutional Convention, likely because it was so similar to the provision in the Articles of Confederation;[33] however, at the convention, James Wilson, a natural law scholar, summarized the provision in the Articles of Consideration as "making the Citizens of one State Citizens of all."[34] A reference in *The Federalist* confirms that the clause, like the provision, was meant to promote comity[35] and specifically "the equal treatment of citizens."[36] Given this history, the U.S. Supreme Court has described the clause as merely a shorter version of the provision,[37] although scholars have noted a few key differences of little relevance for the purpose of

31. ARTICLES OF CONFEDERATION OF 1781, art. IV, ¶ 1.

32. Douglass v. Stephens, 1 Del. Ch. 465, 469 (1821).

33. David S. Bogen, *The Privileges and Immunities Clause of Article IV*, 37 CASE W. RES. L. REV. 794, 840 (1987).

34. *Madison Debates* (Aug. 13, 1787), AVALON PROJECT, https://avalon.law.yale.edu/18th_century/debates_813.asp#1.

35. THE FEDERALIST NO. 80 (Alexander Hamilton) (calling the clause "the basis of the Union").

36. BARNETT & BERNICK, *supra* note 15, at 56.

37. Austin v. New Hampshire, 420 U.S. 656, 660–61 (1975).

this article (e.g., the Article IV Clause has been called more "egalitarian" because "[i]t removed the exclusion of 'paupers' and 'vagabonds'").[38]

The Article IV Clause, on its face, and given its history and purpose, could be read to effectively prohibit all discrimination by a state in favor of its own residents; however, in an early decision, *Corfield v. Coryell*, a Justice riding circuit construed the clause to protect only some "fundamental" rights.[39] New Jersey prohibited nonresidents from "taking oysters" within its waters, which the court concluded was not a right protected by the clause because "[t]he oyster beds . . . might be totally exhausted and destroyed if the [state] legislature could not so regulate the use of them. . . ."[40] The court, however, provided an expansive, nonexclusive list of rights protected by the clause:

> Protection by the government; the enjoyment of life and liberty, with the right to ac-
> quire and possess property of every kind, and to pursue and obtain happiness and
> safety; subject nevertheless to such restraints as the government may justly prescribe
> for the general good of the whole. The right of a citizen of one state to pass through,
> or to reside in any other state, for purposes of trade, agriculture, professional pur-
> suits, or otherwise; to claim the benefit of the writ of habeas corpus; to institute and
> maintain actions of any kind in the courts of the state; to take, hold and dispose of
> property, either real or personal; and an exemption from higher taxes or impositions
> than are paid by the other citizens of the state. . . .[41]

Other decisions similarly use broad language in describing rights protected by the clause, while acknowledging it does not require absolute equal treatment—no one seriously thinks that a state could not prohibit nonresidents from voting in state elections, for example.[42]

Corfield has been exceedingly influential; it has been described as a "landmark opin-ion" by two scholars.[43] Another scholar went so far as to say, hyperbolically, that "every

---

38. BARNETT & BERNICK, *supra* note 15, at 55.

39. Corfield v. Coryell, 6 F. Cas. 546, 551 (C.C.E.D. Penn. 1823).

40. *Id.* at 552.

41. *Id.* at 551–52.

42. *See, e.g., Douglass*, 1 Del. Ch. at 468–69; Murray v. McCarty, 16 Va. (2 Munf.) 393, 396–98 (1811) (Cabell, J., seriatim).

43. BARNETT & BERNICK, *supra* note 15, at 44.

court paid homage to its fundamental rights interpretation of the clause."[44] Notably, *Corfield* is hardly ever cited for its specific conclusion about taking oysters; instead, it is generally cited for the broad list of rights the court concluded were protected by the clause.

Consistent with *Corfield*, to this day, Article IV Clause jurisprudence requires a "two-step" analysis: (1) determine if a right is within the purview of the clause (a lot of rights are); and then (2) determine whether the state is discriminating in favor of its own residents, and if it is, whether the degree of differing treatment is justifiable—that is, whether it promotes "a substantial state interest."[45] Step 2 has been described as "at least as demanding as intermediate scrutiny," a test developed to deal with sex discrimination.[46]

Notably, not everyone has agreed that the Article IV Clause is about discrimination.[47] A particularly important figure in the mid-nineteenth century had a different understanding of the Article IV Clause. Representative John Bingham, who would later become the primary drafter of the Fourteenth Amendment Clause, gave a speech in 1859 opposing Oregon's admission to the Union—he was primarily concerned about racist provisions within the proposed state constitution.[48] These provisions applied to the detriment of not just nonresidents but also Black residents.[49] Representative Bingham argued that these provisions violated the Article IV Clause, which he said should be read as follows: "The citizens of each State shall be entitled to all privileges and immunities of citizens [of the United States] in the several States." This understanding of the clause is particularly relevant to this article, as Representative Bingham would go on to use the phrase "privileges or immunities of citizens of the United States" in drafting the Fourteenth Amendment Clause.[50] In his words,

---

44. Chester James Antieau, *Paul's Perverted Privileges or the True Meaning of the Privileges and Immunities Clause of Article Four*, 9 WM. & MARY L. REV. 1, 12 (1967).

45. *Friedman*, 487 U.S. at 64–65; *see also Toomer*, 334 U.S. at 396.

46. Julian N. Eule, *Laying the Dormant Commerce Clause to Rest*, 91 YALE L.J. 425, 454 (1982).

47. *See generally* Antieau, *supra* note 44.

48. John Bingham, *Speech Opposing the Admission of Oregon* (1859), *in* 1 THE RECONSTRUCTION AMENDMENTS: THE ESSENTIAL DOCUMENTS 152, 152 (Kurt T. Lash ed., 2021).

49. *Id.*

50. *See infra* Part II.

The citizens of each State, all the citizens of each State, being citizens of the United States, shall be entitled to "all privileges and immunities of the citizens in the several States." Not to the rights and immunities of the several States; not to those constitutional rights and immunities which result exclusively from State authority or State legislation; but to "all privileges and immunities" of citizens of the United States in the several States. There is an ellipsis in the language employed in the Constitution, but its meaning is self-evident that it is "the privileges and immunities of citizens of the United States in the several States" that it guaranties.[51]

Consistent with *Corfield*, Representative Bingham also described the rights protected using broad language, referencing "natural rights" four times.[52] He described "natural rights" as "those rights common to all men, and to protect which, not to confer, all good governments are instituted. . . ."[53] He then explained, "I cannot . . . consent that the majority of any republican State may, in any way, rightfully restrict the humblest citizen of the United States in the free exercise of any one of his natural rights. . . ."[54] He explicitly referenced the "the right . . . to work and enjoy the product of . . . toil" as "the rock on which the Constitution rests."[55]

Representative Bingham did not persuade his colleagues, and Oregon became a state, with its discriminatory constitution unchanged.[56] His speech, however, supports the argument that he (as the primary drafter of the Fourteenth Amendment Clause) wanted natural rights protected—he did not view the "privileges and immunities" of United States citizenship narrowly at all. To him, the Article IV Clause protected the natural rights of all citizens—it was not about state discrimination against nonresidents.

Representative Bingham was not alone in this view, although it was not a widely held position during the nation's early years.[57] Moreover, this expansive view of "privileges

---

51. Bingham, *supra* note 48, at 153.

52. *Id.* at 154–56.

53. *Id.* at 156.

54. *Id.*

55. *Id.*

56. *Id.* at 156 n.*.

57. BARNETT & BERNICK, *supra* note 15, at 57. *Contra* Richard L. Aynes, *Constricting the Law of Freedom: Justice Miller, the Fourteenth Amendment, and the Slaughter-House Cases*, 70 CHI.-KENT L. REV. 627, 636 (1994) (claiming "while *Corfield* had up to that time been generally understood to protect the rights

and immunities" became more prominent around the time that the Fourteenth Amendment Clause came into existence.[58]

Notably, in the infamous *Dred Scott v. Sandford* decision, the U.S. Supreme Court endorsed this reading, decrying that if Black people could be citizens of the United States, then they would have substantive constitutional rights under the Article IV Clause, including the right to sue in federal court.[59] In the Court's view, the phrase "citizens in the several states" meant "people of the United States" in the several states, and Black people were not among "this people."[60] The Court expressly decided that a citizen of one state may "not be entitled to the rights and privileges of a citizen in any other State" because the Article IV Clause protects only a "citizen of the United States."[61] The Court reached an abhorrent outcome based on consequentialist reasoning; however, as one scholar stated, "[I]sn't it beyond dubiety" that even the *Dred Scott* Court thought "the privileges and immunities" protected by the clause were not about discriminatory treatment?[62] In other words, if the Article IV Clause did not protect fundamental rights, then why was the Court concerned about whether Black people could make use of it? Obviously, the *Dred Scott* Court was concerned about the power of the clause and its ability to confer rights on Black people.

In 1868, the U.S. Supreme Court, in *Paul v. Virginia*, indicated that the Article IV Clause does not protect all citizens' substantive fundamental rights but rather those rights recognized by the state in question (although it did not address *Dred Scott*).[63] Despite some scholarly criticism,[64] the validity of this portion of *Paul* has not been seriously questioned by the Court; accordingly, as already explained, while many rights are within the Article IV Clause's purview, discriminatory treatment is necessary for a successful claim.

---

of national citizens, . . . [the U.S. Supreme Court in *Slaughter-House*] made it appear that it had protected rights of state citizens").

58. *See infra* Part II.

59. Dred Scott v. Sandford, 60 U.S. (19 How.) 393, 403–07 (1857), *superseded by* U.S. Const. amend. XIV, § 1.

60. *Id.* at 404, 406.

61. *Id.* at 405.

62. Antieau, *supra* note 44, at 12.

63. Paul v. Virginia, 75 U.S. (8 Wall.) 168, 180 (1868), *overruled on other grounds*, United States v. Se. Underwriters Ass'n, 322 U.S. 533 (1944).

64. Antieau, *supra* note 44.

Even still, the U.S. Supreme Court has a long history of declaring various statutes that burden the right to earn a living unenforceable under the Article IV Clause. In 1871—just a few years after the Fourteenth Amendment was adopted—the U.S. Supreme Court held unenforceable a state law that required nonresidents to pay more for a license to trade in foreign goods.[65] As the Court stated in this seminal decision, "[T]he clause plainly and unmistakably secures and protects the right of a citizen of one State to pass into any other State of the Union for the purpose of engaging in lawful commerce, trade, or business without molestation. . . ."[66]

In 1948, in *Toomer v. Witsell*, the U.S. Supreme Court held unconstitutional a state law that required nonresidents to pay more for a commercial fishing license.[67] The Court focused on the step 2 analysis (whether the degree of discriminatory treatment was justifiable), considering step 1 well settled by existing precedent: "In line with . . . [the Article IV Clause's] purpose, it was long ago decided that one of the privileges which the clause guarantees to citizens of State A is that of doing business in State B on terms of substantial equality with the citizens of that State."[68] The Court did not address *Corfield*, but its holding indicates that the *Corfield* court's specific conclusion about taking oysters was incorrect.

In 1952, the U.S. Supreme Court held invalid a scheme in the Alaska Territory that required nonresidents to pay more for a commercial fishing license even though it was not a state.[69] Technically, the decision was not about the Article IV Clause but rather a federal statute; however, the Court "presumed" that Congress would not have authorized a territory to treat nonresidents worse, discussing *Toomer* at length.[70]

In 1978, the U.S. Supreme Court held unconstitutional a statute that required residents to be given preferential hiring treatment for positions in the oil and gas industry.[71] In this decision, the Court used some of its clearest language about the right to earn a living:

---

65. Ward v. Maryland, 79 U.S. 418 (1871).

66. *Id.* at 430.

67. *Toomer*, 334 U.S. at 395.

68. *Id.* at 396.

69. Mullaney v. Anderson, 342 U.S. 415 (1952).

70. *Id.* at 417–20.

71. Hicklin v. Orbeck, 437 U.S. 518 (1978).

"Appellants' appeal to the protection of the [c]lause is strongly supported by this Court's decisions holding violative of the [c]lause state discrimination against nonresidents seeking to ply their trade, practice their occupation, or pursue a common calling within the State."[72]

In 1984, the U.S. Supreme Court reversed a judgment of a state supreme court because the state court had reasoned that the Article IV Clause was inapplicable to a municipal ordinance requiring 40 percent of "the employees of contractors and subcontractors working on city construction projects be" residents of the municipality.[73] The municipality, the City of Camden, New Jersey, is located right on the border of Philadelphia, Pennsylvania, which made the state court's reasoning that the "ordinance discriminates on the basis of municipal, not state, residency," seem absurd; the U.S. Supreme Court strongly condemned any distinction between state and municipal law for the purpose of deciding Article IV Clause claims.[74] The Court said that "[m]any, if not most," of its precedents on the Article IV Clause have dealt with "the pursuit of a common calling," which the Court characterized as a "basic and essential activity."[75] "Public employment," the Court held, was merely "a subspecies of the broader opportunity to pursue a common calling."[76]

In the last two decades, several lower courts have recognized the importance of the Article IV Clause in protecting economic liberty, including the right to earn a living. For example, in 2002, the District of Massachusetts enjoined an ordinance that required 50 percent of construction work hours on public works projects to be performed by city residents, noting that "[i]t is the purpose of the [Article IV] Clause to protect . . . the rights of citizens to pursue a common calling. . . ."[77]

72. *Id.* at 524.
73. *United Bldg.*, 465 U.S. at 210.
74. *Id.* at 210, 215–16.
75. *Id.* at 219.
76. *Id.*
77. Utility Contractors Ass'n of New England, Inc. v. City of Worcester, 236 F. Supp. 2d 113, 117 (D. Mass. 2002).

In 2003, Connecticut residents challenged a "[n]onresident Lobster Law" in New York, which affected their "lawful pursuit of livelihood—commercial lobstering."[78] The Second Circuit agreed with their claim that the law violated the Article IV Clause.[79]

More recently, in *Brusznicki v. Prince George's County*, a 2022 decision, the Fourth Circuit considered a Maryland statute that directed counties "to offer defaulted properties to a select class of people (comprising largely those living and holding government positions there) before listing the properties for regular public auction."[80] Three plaintiffs "in the business of purchasing tax-lien certificates" and who were not in that class sued, claiming the statute violated the Article IV Clause.[81] They argued the statute violated their "fundamental rights to own property and pursue a chosen profession"—the Fourth Circuit agreed.[82] In its words, "Plaintiffs wish to purchase property largely for commercial ends," which fell within "the right to a common calling" as "broadly" conceptualized in Article IV Clause jurisprudence.[83]

In summary, while much may be unclear about the Article IV Clause, one thing is clear: at step 1, the clause protects economic liberty, including the right to earn a living.[84]

These decisions often emphasize that economic liberty is critical to the national economy, which is in turn critical to national unity. In *Supreme Court of New Hampshire v. Piper*, a 1985 decision, the U.S. Supreme Court said that an attorney has a "fundamental right" to "practice law" that is protected by the Article IV Clause.[85] It emphasized the role that attorneys play in the "national economy," noting that "activities of lawyers play an important part in commercial intercourse."[86] Three years later, in *Friedman*, the Court summarized its decision in *Piper* as applicable to "other occupations," so long as they are "sufficiently basic to the national economy to be deemed a privilege protected by the

---

78. Connecticut ex rel. Blumenthal v. Crotty, 346 F.3d 84, 89, 96 (2d Cir. 2003).

79. *Id.* at 88.

80. Brusznicki v. Prince George's County, 42 F.4th 413, 416 (4th Cir. 2022).

81. *Id.* at 416–17.

82. *Id.* at 417.

83. *Id.* at 421–22.

84. Bogen, *supra* note 33, at 831, 856.

85. Sup. Ct. of N.H. v. Piper, 470 U.S. 274, 281 (1985).

86. *Id.* (quoting Goldfarb v. Va. State Bar, 421 U.S. 773, 788 (1975)).

[c]lause."[87] References to the national economy permeate Article IV Clause jurisprudence and, as discussed below, echo the language of *Slaughter-House*.[88]

II. AN OVERVIEW OF THE FOURTEENTH AMENDMENT CLAUSE

The Fourteenth Amendment Clause was added as a part of the Reconstruction Amendments after the Civil War and was based on the Article IV Clause. The drafting history demonstrates that the framers of the Fourteenth Amendment believed that the phrase "Privileges and Immunities of citizens in the several States," which appears in the Article IV Clause, was not measurably different from "privileges or immunities of citizens of the United States," the phrase used in the Fourteenth Amendment Clause.

After the Civil War, the federal government tried to protect former slaves from oppressive state action.[89] Congress enacted the Civil Rights Act of 1866, which promised Black citizens "full and equal benefit of all laws and proceedings for the security of person and property, as is enjoyed by white citizens," among other things such as the right to make and enforce contracts free of racial discrimination.[90] Southern states had passed laws, so-called Black Codes, restraining Black people from earning a living (among other things), and according to one scholar, Congress's "primary concern" in passing the Act was to protect the "economic rights . . . [of] new black citizens."[91] Another scholar said that the Act "enshrined free labor values as part of the definition of American citizenship."[92]

Opponents of the Civil Rights Act argued that Congress lacked the authority to enact it, which sparked discussions about the need for a constitutional amendment.[93]

---

87. *Friedman*, 487 U.S. at 66.

88. *See also Hicklin*, 437 U.S. at 531–32.

89. McDonald v. City of Chicago, 561 U.S. 742, 771–75 (2010).

90. 14 Stat. 27, § 1 (1866), *codified as amended*, 42 U.S.C. § 1981.

91. Sandefur, *supra* 3, at 227–28; *see also* ERIC FONER, THE SECOND FOUNDING 48 (2019) (explaining Black people were prohibited from entering "certain occupations"); ERIC FONER, FREE SOIL, FREE LABOR, FREE MEN xxxv (1995) (calling the Civil Rights Act a partial "response to . . . Black Codes that severely limited the liberty of former slaves").

92. FONER, FREE SOIL, *supra* 91, at xxxv.

93. *See* Students for Fair Admissions, Inc. v. President & Fellows of Harvard Coll., 600 U.S. 181, 234–38 (2023) (Thomas, J., concurring).

Discussions about a constitutional amendment were ongoing even before the Civil Rights Act was enacted in April 1866, given concerns about the Act's validity. In February of that year, a few representatives, including Representative Bingham, argued in favor of a proposed constitutional amendment allowing Congress "to secure to the citizens of each State all privileges and immunities of citizens in the several States"—language taken directly from the Article IV Clause.[94] The proposed amendment was "intended to enable Congress by its enactments when necessary to give to a citizen of the United States, in whatever State he may be, those privileges and immunities which are guaranteed to him under the Constitution of the United States."[95] One representative emphasized that it would empower Congress "to give to all citizens the inalienable rights of life and liberty. . . ."[96] In speaking, Representative Bingham equated the language used in the Article IV Clause with the language that would eventually be used in the Fourteenth Amendment Clause: "[The proposed amendment] secures to the citizens of each of the States all the privileges and immunities of citizens of the several States. . . . It is to secure to the citizen of each State all the privileges and immunities of citizens of the United States in the several States."[97] Effectively, "citizens in the Several States" meant, in his view, "citizens of the United States"—a view he had expressed years earlier in opposing Oregon's admission to the Union. This proposal failed to garner sufficient votes. Notably, just a few years after the Fourteenth Amendment was ratified, Representative Bingham said that the "rights, privileges, and immunities" of United States citizenship include "the liberty . . . to work in an honest calling and contribute by your toil in some sort to the support of yourself, to the support of your fellow-men, and to be secure in the enjoyment of the fruits of your toil."[98] Similarly, post ratification, a senator remarked:

94. *US House, Debate Continued, "Privileges and Immunities" Amendment, Speeches of John Bingham and Giles Hotchkiss, Vote to Postpone Consideration* (1866), *in* 2 THE RECONSTRUCTION AMENDMENTS, *supra* note 48, at 108, 109.

95. *Id.* at 109.

96. *Id.*

97. *Id.* at 117.

98. *US House, Speech of John Bingham on the Meaning of the Privileges or Immunities Clause of Section One of the Fourteenth Amendment* (1871), *in* 2 THE RECONSTRUCTION AMENDMENTS, *supra* note 48, at 620, 629.

"Has not every person a right to carry on his own occupation, to secure the fruits of his own industry, and appropriate them as best suits himself . . . ?"[99]

In May 1866, when the House of Representatives debated the language that would ultimately become the Fourteenth Amendment, Representative Bingham argued that the purpose of the Fourteenth Amendment Clause was to remediate violations of the Article IV Clause: "No State ever had the right, under the forms of law or otherwise, to . . . abridge the privileges or immunities of any citizen of the Republic, although many of them have assumed and exercised the power, and that without a remedy."[100] The assumption underlying this argument is that the rights protected by the Article IV Clause are largely the same—if not exactly the same—as those protected under the Fourteenth Amendment Clause.

During the Senate debate, that same month, one senator explained that when the Constitution was initially drafted, there was no such thing as a citizen of the United States—although he acknowledged that phrase appeared in parts of the Constitution as originally drafted.[101] To him, the point of the Article IV Clause "was to constitute *ipso facto* the citizens of each of the original States citizens of the United States."[102] In discussing what these rights of United States citizenship under the Article IV Clause might be, he quoted the long list of rights from *Corfield*.[103] In his view, the primary if not sole reason for passing the Fourteenth Amendment Clause was to ensure that the federal government could effectively safeguard the rights he thought were already protected by the Article IV Clause (and, to the extent not clearly expressed in Article IV Clause jurisprudence, to incorporate the Bill of Rights against the states).[104] This speech has been called a particularly "direct[]" statement about the clause's original understanding because it was "widely disseminated."[105]

---

99. 2 Cong. Rec. app. 363 (1874).

100. *US House, Proposed Fourteenth Amendment, Debate and Passage* (1866), in 2 The Reconstruction Amendments, *supra* note 48, at 170, 178.

101. *US Senate, Proposed Fourteenth Amendment, Speech of Jacob Howard Introducing the Amendment*, in 2 The Reconstruction Amendments, *supra* note 48, at 186, 186–87.

102. *Id.* at 186.

103. *Id.*

104. *Id.* at 187–88.

105. Barnett & Bernick, *supra* note 15, at 140.

A Massachusetts legislative committee during the ratification debate similarly understood the Fourteenth Amendment Clause as analogous to—if not functionally the same as—the Article IV Clause.[106] The committee noted, "[W]e are not aware that there has been any decision, or that there is any agreement among legal authorities as to what constitutes citizenship of a State, apart from citizenship in the United States."[107] The committee declared most of Section 1 of the Fourteenth Amendment "at best, mere surplusage."[108] The committee was concerned that Section 1 could be understood to imply that already existing rights actually did not exist.[109]

A similar concern was raised in a Maryland legislative committee report, which quoted the Article IV Clause and noted that a "citizen of a State" is a "citizen of the United States."[110] Interestingly, both those in favor of and in opposition to the Fourteenth Amendment appeared to agree that the Article IV Clause protected a very similar set of rights. One Maryland resident in opposition even declared, "[U]nder the Constitution, independent of this supposed amendment, the provisions as to the rights of citizens are the same as those of the amendment."[111]

Newspapers at the time also described the rights of "citizen[s] of the United States" using the broad language that had been previously used in reference to the Article IV Clause. In one article, the author argued, "[The people] demand and will have protection for every citizen of the United States, everywhere within the national jurisdiction— *full and complete protection* in the enjoyment of life, liberty, property, the pursuit of happiness, the right to speak and write his sentiments, regardless of localities; to keep and bear arms in his own defence . . ." (emphasis added).[112] Later in the same article, the

---

106. *Massachusetts, Legislative Committee on Federal Relations, Majority and Minority Reports on the Proposed Fourteenth Amendment* (1867), in 2 THE RECONSTRUCTION AMENDMENTS, *supra* note 48, 383, 384.

107. *Id.* at 385.

108. *Id.*

109. *Id.*

110. *Maryland, Legislature's Joint Committee Report, Rejection of the Fourteenth Amendment*, in 2 THE RECONSTRUCTION AMENDMENTS, *supra* note 48, at 393, 395.

111. *Reverdy Johnson, "A Further Consideration of the Dangerous Conditions of the County,"* in 2 THE RECONSTRUCTION AMENDMENTS, *supra* note 48 at 403, 403.

112. *"Madison," Essays on the Fourteenth Amendment, Nos. I, II, and V, New York Times* (1866), in 2 THE RECONSTRUCTION AMENDMENTS, *supra* note 48, at 297, 297.

author said that the long list of rights from *Corfield* are "the long-defined rights of a citizen of the United States, with which States cannot constitutionally interfere."[113] Another newspaper article from the same author said that the purpose of the Fourteenth Amendment Clause was merely to let the federal government enforce the Article IV Clause.[114]

Accordingly, a review of the historical record confirms that the Fourteenth Amendment Clause was not originally understood to protect a different—and narrower—set of rights than the Article IV Clause. In the primary sources, the references to the Article IV Clause and specifically *Corfield* are simply too many to ignore—not to mention, several of the references to the Article IV Clause discuss a much broader understanding of that clause than recognized in modern jurisprudence. In fact, Justice Clarence Thomas has stated that "*Corfield* indisputably influenced the Members of Congress who enacted the Fourteenth Amendment[.] Members frequently, if not as a matter of course, appealed to *Corfield*, arguing that the Amendment was necessary to guarantee the fundamental rights . . . identified in . . . [the] opinion."[115] Additionally, "it appears that no member of Congress refuted the notion that . . . [the] analysis in *Corfield* undergirded the meaning of the" Fourteenth Amendment Clause.[116] The history of the Civil Rights Act and its relation to the Fourteenth Amendment Clause also confirms that the clause was at least in part about safeguarding economic liberty. Scholars generally agree that the Fourteenth Amendment Clause's original understanding "guarantee[d] and constitutionalize[d]" the rights safeguarded by the Act.[117]

Despite the historical record, the two clauses are currently interpreted very differently because of the decision in *Slaughter-House*. Shortly after the Fourteenth Amendment was ratified, *Slaughter-House* commenced in the District Court for Louisiana.[118] Louisiana enacted a law in 1869 that gave one private company—the Crescent City Livestock Landing & Slaughterhouse Company—a monopoly to slaughter animals in the New Orleans

113. *Id.* at 298–99.

114. *Id.* at 299.

115. Saenz v. Roe, 526 U.S. 489, 526 (1999) (Thomas, J., dissenting).

116. *Id.*

117. Sandefur, *supra* note 3, at 228 (quoting BERNARD H. SEIGAN, ECONOMIC LIBERTIES AND THE CONSTITUTION 50 (1980)); *see also* BARNETT & BERNICK, *supra* note 15, at 144.

118. Live-Stock Dealers' & Butchers' Ass'n v. Crescent City Live-Stock Landing & Slaughter-House Co., 15 F. Cas. 649 (C.C.D. La. 1870), *rev'd*, *Slaughter-House*, 83 U.S. 36.

vicinity.[119] The law stated, "[A]ll . . . [livestock] shall be landed at the stock-landings and slaughtered at the slaughterhouses of the company, and nowhere else."[120] The law literally referred to this right as an "exclusive privilege."[121] An association of butchers sued, arguing the law violated the Fourteenth Amendment Clause by "creating a monopoly . . . conferring odious and exclusive privileges upon a small number of persons at the expense of the great body of the community" and "depriv[ing] a large and meritorious class of citizens—the whole of the butchers of the city—of the right to exercise their trade, the business to which they have been trained and on which they depend for the support of themselves and their families. . . ."[122]

The district court ruled in favor of the association, concluding, "[I]t would be difficult to conceive of a more flagrant case of violation of the fundamental rights of labor than the one before us."[123] As it articulated, "[T]he citizen has chosen a lawful and useful employment. He has been brought up to it, and educated in it. He has invested property in it. He is willing to comply with all police regulations, properly such, in the exercise of it."[124] Under such circumstances, the butchers had a constitutional right to practice their chosen profession, in the court's view.[125]

The U.S. Supreme Court reversed in a 5–4 decision.[126] The Court spent little time addressing the historical record, but it did try to distinguish the text of the Article IV Clause from the text of the Fourteenth Amendment Clause[127] (albeit while misquoting the Article IV Clause).[128] As it reasoned, the Article IV Clause "embrace[s] . . . civil rights[s] for

119. *See Slaughter-House*, 83 U.S. at 59.

120. *Id.*

121. *Id.*

122. *Id.* at 60.

123. *Live-Stock Dealers' & Butchers' Ass'n*, 15 F. Cas. at 653.

124. *Id.* at 654.

125. *Id.*

126. *Slaughter-House*, 83 U.S. 36.

127. *Id.* at 75–79.

128. Notably, the U.S. Supreme Court in *Slaughter-House* misquoted the Article IV Clause as follows: "The citizens of each State shall be entitled to all the privileges and immunities of citizens *of* the several States." *Id.* at 75 (emphasis added). The actual language of the clause does not say "of the several States" but rather "in the several States." U.S. CONST. art. IV, § 2. Even left-leaning scholars, who may not like an expansive view of economic liberty, have acknowledged that the misquotation is significant because it totally avoids the expansive reading of the Article IV Clause that had been offered by

the establishment and protection of which organized governments is instituted"—that is, natural rights.[129] As explained above, that conclusion is correct: the Article IV Clause was designed to protect a large group of fundamental rights. Then, however, the Court took a very narrow view of the Fourteenth Amendment Clause, holding that the clause only protected rights that stem from the "National character" of the federal government.[130] The Court gave a few examples, including (1) the right to access seaports, "through which all operations of foreign commerce are conducted," (2) the right to "come to the seat of government" to transact business and assert claims, and (3) the right to demand "protection of the Federal Government over his life, liberty, and property when on the high seas or within the jurisdiction of a foreign government."[131]

Three strong dissents were authored in *Slaughter-House*. The lead dissent, joined by four Justices, explained that while a state "may prescribe such regulations for every pursuit and calling of life as will promote the public health, secure the good order and advance the general prosperity of society," it could not ban anyone willing to follow these regulations from working in a common calling.[132] This distinction, between regulating and prohibiting, was also discussed in another dissent: "[T]he right of any citizen to follow whatever lawful employment he chooses to adopt (submitting himself to all lawful regulations) is one which the legislature of a State cannot invade, whether restrained by its own constitution or not."[133] The third dissent, echoing the philosopher John Locke, explained, "[L]abor is property, and as such merits protection."[134]

Representative Bingham and others. James W. Fox, Jr., *Re-Readings and Misreadings: Slaughter-House, Privileges or Immunities, and Section Five Enforcement Powers*, 91 KY. L.J. 67, 80 (2002). If Representative Bingham was right, and the Article IV Clause should be read as "citizens of the United States in the several States," the entire basis for the Court's textual distinction breaks down. Representative Bingham's reading would be wholly meritless if the Article IV Clause explicitly referred to "citizens of the several States." *See supra* Part I.

129. *Slaughter-House*, 83 U.S. at 76.

130. *Id.* at 79.

131. *Id.*

132. *Id.* at 110 (Fields, J., dissenting).

133. *Id.* at 113–14 (Bradley, J., dissenting).

134. *Compare id.* at 127 (Swayne, J., dissenting), *with* JOHN LOCKE, SECOND TREATISE ON GOVERNMENT § 27 (1689) ("The *Labour* of his Body, and the *Work* of his Hands, we may say, are properly his. . . . For this *Labour* being the unquestionable Property of the Labourer, no man but he can have a right to what that is once joyned to. . . .").

Notably, the dissenters refused to recognize the validity of *Slaughter-House*, with one writing just a few years later that "[t]he right to follow any of the common occupations of life is an inalienable right."[135] As the Justice continued, "to deny it to all but a few favored individuals, by investing the latter with a monopoly, is to invade one of the fundamental privileges of the citizen, contrary not only to common right, but . . . to the express words of the [C]onstitution."[136] Another wrote that the Fourteenth Amendment Clause "recognized, if it did not create, a National citizenship . . . and declared that their privileges and immunities, which embrace fundamental rights belonging to citizens of all free governments, should not be abridged by the State."[137]

The dissents were even relied upon in the lower courts, perhaps most famously in *In re Parrott*, a decision from the District of California in 1880.[138] The decision dealt, in part, with the Burlingame Treaty between the United States and China, which provided for "the free immigration and emigration of citizens and subjects" of both nations for "purposes of curiosity, or trade, or as permanent residents."[139] The next article of the treaty declared that citizens of both nations "shall enjoy the same privileges, immunities, and exemptions, in respect to travel or residence, as may there be enjoyed by the citizens or subjects of the most favored nation."[140] California claimed, as a matter of police powers, that it could prohibit corporations from hiring Chinese people, regardless of the treaty.[141] The court disagreed.[142] To construe the treaty, it looked first to *Corfield* and then to other Article IV Clause decisions.[143] It then quoted both the majority and dissents in *Slaughter-House*.[144] As the court explained, "Some of these extracts are from the dissenting opinions, but not upon points where there is any disagreement. There is no difference of

135. Butchers' Union Slaughter-House & Live-Stock Landing Co. v. Crescent City Live-Stock Landing & Slaughter-House Co., 111 U.S. 746, 762 (1884) (Bradley, J., concurring).

136. *Id.*

137. Bartemeyer v. Iowa, 85 U.S. (18 Wall.) 129, 140 (1873) (Field, J., concurring).

138. *In re* Parrott, 1 F. 481 (C.C.D. Cal. 1880).

139. *Id.* at 485.

140. *Id.* at 504.

141. *Id.* at 484.

142. *Id.* at 504.

143. *Id.*

144. *Id.* at 505–06.

opinion as to the significance of the terms 'privileges and immunities.'"[145] "Indeed," the court continued, "it seems quite impossible that any definition of these terms could be adopted, or even seriously proposed, so narrow as to exclude the right to labor for subsistence."[146]

Evidently, the decision in *Slaughter-House* has been controversial since the day it was rendered. A prominent law professor, Richard A. Epstein, has said that "[i]n the eyes of virtually all historians, there is little doubt that *Slaughter-House* is wrong."[147]

In 2010, the U.S. Supreme Court recognized that *Slaughter-House* was likely decided incorrectly, quoting the work of another law professor who said that "virtually no serious scholar—left, right, and center—thinks . . . [*Slaughter-House*] is a plausible reading."[148] In the 2010 decision, the Court was asked to incorporate the Second Amendment's right to keep and bear arms against the states via the Fourteenth Amendment Clause.[149] A plurality of the Court declined, claiming that while many scholars agreed *Slaughter-House* was wrong, less agreement existed on whether the right to keep and bear arms was a privilege or immunity; instead, the Court relied on the Due Process Clause of the Fourteenth Amendment for incorporation, negating a need to revisit *Slaughter-House*.[150] (As an aside, a few primary sources explicitly indicate that the right to keep and bear arms is protected by the Fourteenth Amendment Clause.)[151]

---

145. *Id.* at 506.

146. *Id.*

147. Richard A. Epstein, *Further Thoughts on the Privileges or Immunities Clause of the Fourteenth Amendment*, 1 N.Y.U. J.L. & LIBERTY 1096, 1098 (2005).

148. *McDonald*, 561 U.S. at 756 (quoting Akhil Reed Amar, *Substance and Method in the Year 2000*, 28 PEPP. L. REV. 601, 631 n.178 (2001)).

149. *Id.* at 758.

150. *Id.* (plurality opinion); *see also id.* at 805–06 (Thomas, J., concurring in part & concurring in the judgment) (explaining the Court should have relied upon the Fourteenth Amendment Clause).

151. *E.g., Madison, supra* note 112, at 297, 299 (explaining each of "the people" demands the right "to keep and bear arms in his own defence" and then referring to this right as a "privilege" safeguarded by the Article IV Clause, which would become better protected by the Fourteenth Amendment Clause); *see also* JOHN TIFFANY, A TREATISE ON THE UNCONSTITUTIONALITY OF AMERICAN SLAVERY (1849), *in* 1 THE RECONSTRUCTION AMENDMENTS, *supra* note 48, at 237, 251 (referring to the right to keep and bear arms as "another of the immunities of a citizen of the United States, which is guaranteed by the supreme organic law of the land" and arguing "[t]he colored citizen, under our constitution, has now as full and perfect a right to keep and bear arms as any other").

In 2023, the U.S. Supreme Court denied a petition for certiorari explicitly asking it to overrule *Slaughter-House*.[152] Ursula Newell-Davis, a social worker, wanted to engage in "respite care"—that is, "short-term relief to primary caregivers of special needs children."[153] In Louisiana, respite work is regulated, and an applicant "must undergo what's called a facility Need Review."[154] This process does not look at an applicant's qualifications but rather whether a provider is "needed" in light of the total amount of work in the community.[155] Louisiana did not even try to defend its regulation on public safety grounds, instead saying that the scheme was implemented to "eas[e] its regulatory burden."[156] Ms. Newell-Davis was rejected not based on her qualifications, but effectively because regulators did not want to have to supervise her business. She lost at the district court and the circuit court because of *Slaughter-House*. The U.S. Supreme Court's denial of her petition demonstrates it is extraordinarily skeptical of the Fourteenth Amendment Clause, perhaps because the clause could be misused as a judicial license to create all kinds of new constitutional rights.[157]

Today, the Fourteenth Amendment Clause is not understood to protect much, but it does protect the "right to travel."[158] As articulated by the U.S. Supreme Court in *Saenz v. Roe*, the Article IV Clause protects one "component" of this right: "[B]y virtue of a person's state citizenship, a citizen of one State who travels in other States, intending to return home at the end of his journey, is entitled to enjoy the 'Privileges and Immunities of Citizens in the several States' that he visits."[159] The specific examples mentioned by the *Saenz* Court are noteworthy: the Article IV Clause protects the right to travel for various legitimate purposes, including "obtain[ing] employment" and "engag[ing] in commercial . . . fishing."[160] Another component, "the right of a newly arrived citizen

---

152. *Newell-Davis*, 144 S. Ct. 98.

153. Petition for a Writ of Certiorari, at i, *Newell-Davis*, 144 S. Ct. 98, https://www.supremecourt.gov/DocketPDF/22/22-1208/268914/20230612153454500_Newell-Davis%20Brief_pdfa.pdf.

154. *Id.* at 3.

155. *Id.*

156. *Id.* at i.

157. *See* BARNETT & BERNICK, *supra* note 15, at 42.

158. *Saenz*, 526 U.S. 489 (majority opinion).

159. *Id.* at 501.

160. *Id.* at 502.

to the same privileges and immunities enjoyed by other citizens of the same State," is protected by the Fourteenth Amendment Clause.[161] As stated in *Slaughter-House*, "[A] citizen of the United States can, of his own volition, become a citizen of any State of the Union by a *bona fide* residence therein, with the same rights as other citizens of that State."[162] Notably, the *Saenz* Court quoted one of the dissents from *Slaughter-House* at length, seemingly because the Court felt that it could not rely only upon the majority opinion in *Slaughter-House*, given that opinion's reputation.[163] In sum, it is fair to say that *Saenz* at least loosened up *Slaughter-House*'s cramped reading, and may, in the future, provide fodder for further expanding rights recognized under the Fourteenth Amendment Clause.

III. A LITIGATION STRATEGY

Under *Slaughter-House*, economic liberty is not broadly protected by the Fourteenth Amendment Clause. As explained above, only narrow rights of a "national character" are protected, such as "the right of free access [to] seaports," the "right to use the navigable waters of the United States," and the right to "come to the seat of government . . . to transact any business. . . ."[164]

To be sure, these are narrow categories, but they are a starting point for a litigation strategy. Today, the U.S. Supreme Court appears to recognize that *Slaughter-House* was wrong, but also appears reluctant to overrule *Slaughter-House*. So, it seems litigants must work within the existing doctrinal frameworks and seek incremental changes that will eventually lead to greater protection for economic liberty. Incrementalism, rather than outright reversal, may be the preferred route for some current U.S. Supreme Court Justices, such as Chief Justice John Roberts.[165]

Notably, the *Slaughter-House* categories are similar in that they involve the right to travel, which, as already explained, is protected by both the Article IV Clause and the

---

161. *Id.* at 502.

162. *Id.* at 503 (quoting *Slaughter-House*, 16 U.S. at 80 (majority opinion)).

163. *Id.* at 503–04 (quoting *Slaughter-House*, 16 U.S. at 112–13 (Bradley, J., dissenting)).

164. *Slaughter-House*, 16 U.S. at 76 (majority opinion).

165. Tom Curry, *Robert's Rule: Conservative but Incremental*, NBC NEWS (June 25, 2007), https://www.nbcnews.com/id/wbna19415777.

Fourteenth Amendment Clause.[166] Additionally, the precedent for both clauses recognizes similar concerns. Whereas decisions on the Article IV Clause discuss the "national economy,"[167] decisions on the Fourteenth Amendment Clause discuss rights of a "national character."[168] And it is not too much of a stretch to argue that *Saenz* was chiefly a case about economic liberties, though couched in terms of the right to travel.

Based on these commonalities, this article proposes a two-step litigation strategy aimed at loosening *Slaughter-House* incrementally, with the eventual goal of engrafting the rights-describing language from Article IV Clause decisions into Fourteenth Amendment Clause decisions.

As step 1, public interest litigants should bring more Article IV Clause cases alleging violations of economic liberty. *Brusznicki*, overturning a state law mandating how certain commercial properties are sold (discussed above), is a good example. And the U.S. Supreme Court has already held that the right to earn a living is protected as a "privilege" or "immunity" under the Article IV Clause. As a strategic matter, working within this doctrinal framework may result in rights-describing language that is helpful in mounting future Fourteenth Amendment Clause cases. At worst, several bad protectionist statutes will fall.

For step 1, a great deal of attention should be paid to the type of economic liberty cases brought. The existing overlap between the two doctrinal frameworks largely centers on the right to travel. In *Saenz*, the U.S. Supreme Court explicitly recognized that some aspects of this right (such as traveling to obtain employment) are protected by the Article IV Clause and that other aspects (such as deciding to make a state in which one is located a residence) are protected by the Fourteenth Amendment Clause. Accordingly, the Court is more likely to expand this overlap if it can rely on Article IV Clause decisions with fact patterns involving a right to travel for economic purposes when construing the Fourteenth Amendment Clause. In summary, for step 1, this article recommends bringing not just more Article IV Clause cases, but Article IV Clause cases that could arguably fall under the umbrella of *Slaughter-House* and *Saenz*.

---

166. *McDonald*, 561 U.S. at 809 (Thomas, J., concurring in part & concurring in the judgment) ("[T]he Court has held that the Clause prevents state abridgment of only a handful of rights, such as the right to travel. . . .").

167. *Friedman*, 487 U.S. at 66.

168. *Slaughter-House*, 83 U.S. at 79.

Consider this concrete example: a Wisconsin statute provides that "[n]o guide license for hunting or trapping may be issued to or obtained by any person who is not a resident of this state."[169] Without a license, a person may not "engage or be employed for any compensation to guide, direct or assist any other person in hunting . . . or trapping. . . ."[170] The statute provides that a nonresident who violates this prohibition, "upon such conviction," must forfeit up to $100.[171]

The Wisconsin statute clearly impedes the right to earn a living and discriminates between residents and nonresidents. It makes an arbitrary distinction between a Michigander and a Wisconsinite who live just a few miles apart. The Michigander cannot "ply" his "trade," "practice" his "occupation," or "pursue a common calling within" Wisconsin, solely on the basis of his residency.[172] The statute is analogous to, though actually worse than, the commercial fishing license schemes that the U.S. Supreme Court has held invalid on a few occasions in that it is a total ban—not just a higher fee.[173] Because the statute is a total ban, the state cannot even argue that some degree of differential treatment is justified. Hunting guides also implicate tourism, travel, professional business transactions, navigable waters, and even seaports (all "national" concerns noted in *Slaughter-House* and *Saenz*). Other states have similar, albeit less egregious, prohibitions related to hunting and the right to earn a living. For example, in Michigan, a nonresident cannot act as a bear hunting guide.[174] Additionally, in West Virginia, a nonresident cannot train hunting dogs except during small game season.[175]

To further expand this litigation hypothetical: a public interest law firm could represent a waterfowl hunting guide from Michigan or Minnesota who wants to serve clients within Wisconsin but cannot because of this statute. This guide wishes to use navigable (or perhaps even interstate) waters to conduct his business. The guide could also

169. WIS. STAT. § 29.512(1).

170. *Id.*

171. § 29.512(2).

172. *Hicklin*, 437 U.S. at 524.

173. *See supra* Part I.

174. MICH. WILD LIFE CONSERVATION ORDER, Ch. III, § 3.205(2) (prohibiting nonresidents from being bear hunting guides), https://www.michigan.gov/-/media/Project/Websites/dnr/Documents/Orders/Wildlife -Conservation-Order/ChapterIII.pdf?rev=f9475819704a47c58aa503f67bfe9a64.

175. W. VA. STAT. § 20-2-5(22).

allege that he would use Wisconsin marinas (ports) on navigable waterways. A quick Google search for "Minnesota waterfowl guides" reveals dozens of existing businesses, including some that operate already in multiple states.[176] Bringing such a case would likely result in Wisconsin's law being struck down under the Article IV Clause, but with a fact pattern that raises a plausible argument under the Fourteenth Amendment Clause—even within the cramped confines of *Slaughter-House*, which recognized the importance of navigable waters, and so on.

As another example, the Wisconsin state government employs at least hundreds, if not thousands, of "project position" employees—to be eligible, an applicant must reside within the state.[177] As described above, "public employment" is merely "a subspecies of the broader opportunity to pursue a common calling" under existing Article IV Clause precedent.[178] Accordingly, this residency requirement is also ripe for challenge (though it does not involve some of the facts described in the hypothetical case of the hunting guide).

Step 2 is to bring a nearly identical Fourteenth Amendment Clause case that is at least arguably within the existing *Slaughter-House* framework. For example, the waterfowl guide described above could bring such a claim solely under the Fourteenth Amendment Clause, even without bringing an Article IV Clause claim. The guide could rely on the rights-describing language from the precedent created at step 1. The guide's case would inherently involve a right of a "national character" because it would involve the right to travel, including to ports and on navigable waterways.

Bringing this type of case, in this sequence, would therefore present the difficult question for any court: Why does the waterfowl guide win under Article IV, but not under the Fourteenth Amendment? The answer is clear—the guide should win under both clauses, not only because the text and history of both clauses is similar, but even considering the "national character" limitations of *Slaughter-House*.[179]

---

176. *See, e.g., Minnesota Waterfowl Hunting: Western & Metro Minnesota*, MAXXED OUT GUIDES, https://maxxedoutguides.com/minnesota-hunts/.

177. *See* WIS. STAT. § 230.27(1m)(a).

178. *United Bldg.*, 465 U.S. at 219; *see also* Nelson v. Geringer, 295 F.3d 1082, 1084, 1090 n.8 (10th Cir. 2002) (declaring invalid a requirement that a general officer in the Wyoming National Guard reside within the state, although not grounding its decision in the right to pursue a common calling).

179. Notably, in 1978, the U.S. Supreme Court held that the Article IV Clause does not protect a right to engage in recreational hunting; however, that decision is no bar to this litigation strategy. *Baldwin,*

This two-step litigation strategy is adaptable. Most—if not all—states have residency requirements for certain economic activity. Many cities and counties have similar requirements, which are also subject to liability under the Fourteenth Amendment Clause via 42 U.S.C. § 1983. As an example, Atlanta, Georgia, prohibits out-of-state residents from operating taxicabs.[180] As the ordinance states, applicants must "[b]e a resident, for at least one year immediately preceding the date of application, of the state."[181]Atlanta, for context, is home to the nation's busiest airport, serving tens of millions each year.[182] An Uber driver could not travel from Chattanooga or Birmingham during an especially busy season (for example, a World Series or Super Bowl) to help get people to the airport (which is basically a modern-day seaport as described in *Slaughter-House*).[183] More importantly, even if the driver were to move to Atlanta and declare it his or her home, he or she would have to wait a year, which directly implicates the right discussed in both *Slaughter-House* and *Saenz*: "[A] citizen of the United States can, of his own volition, become a citizen of any State of the Union by a *bona fide* residence therein, with the same rights as other citizens of that State."[184] Even if the driver is not a "*bona fide*" resident of Georgia, he or she should have an Article IV Clause claim. Stated differently, after the driver has moved, either he or she is a resident of Georgia, and need not wait a full year, or he or she is a resident of Tennessee/Alabama. Moreover, nothing would prevent a second out-of-state Uber driver from bringing a second lawsuit, under step 2, alleging only a claim under the Fourteenth Amendment Clause. Again, courts would be presented with the sticky question, why should the Uber driver win under one clause but not the other? Presenting this difficult question should incrementally move the Supreme Court to broaden and eventually abandon *Slaughter-House*.

---

436 U.S. at 380. The decision was not about the right to earn a living—just recreational hunting. *See Blumenthal*, 346 F.3d at 96 ("Reliance on *Baldwin* is misplaced, however, as *Baldwin* involved a challenge to Montana's recreational elk hunting law. . . . The Supreme Court drew a clear line of demarcation between the fundamentally protected nature of a nonresident's pursuit of a livelihood and the minimally protected nature of a nonresident's recreational pursuit.").

180. ATLANTA CODE OF ORDINANCES § 162–77(4).

181. *Id.*

182. Michelle Baran, *These Are the 20 Busiest Airports in the United States*, AFAR (Aug. 9, 2024), https://www.afar.com/magazine/busiest-airports-in-the-us.

183. ATLANTA CODE OF ORDINANCES § 162–76; *see also Looking for Driving Jobs in Atlanta, GA?*, UBER, https://www.uber.com/us/en/e/drive/atlanta-ga-us/.

184. *Saenz*, 526 U.S. at 503 (quoting *Slaughter-House*, 16 U.S. at 80).

CONCLUSION

This litigation strategy is viable for several reasons. First, as a matter of originalism, the Fourteenth Amendment Clause's meaning should be tied to the Article IV Clause. The primary sources already discussed are by no means exhaustive, and the meaning of these clauses is often debated; however, one thing is clear: they were not understood to cover largely different sets of rights. Second, the U.S. Supreme Court in *Piper* and other Article IV Clause decisions employed broad language in describing the rights protected by the clause, including express references to the right to earn a living. These cases are consistent with *Corfield*. Third, *Slaughter-House* emphasized the "National character" of the federal government, even noting that rights protected by the Fourteenth Amendment Clause include a right to access seaports.[185] This reasoning is quite similar to the justification for protecting economic liberty under the Article IV Clause: as the Court noted in *Piper*, some occupations implicate the "national economy," and the point of the Article IV Clause was to make the nation unified for economic and other purposes.[186] Protecting the "national economy" is both a matter of national unity (an Article IV Clause concern) and a matter of relevance to the "character" of the federal government, which has substantial control over regulation of interstate commerce (a Fourteenth Amendment Clause concern). Incrementalism may very well be key to protecting economic liberty over the long term.

185. *Slaughter-House*, 83 U.S. at 76.

186. *Piper*, 470 U.S. at 281.

Overtaking the Gatekeepers: Antitrust Law as a Tool to Break Up the Licensing Cartels

By Joshua Polk, Stephen Slivinski, and Caleb Trotter*

INTRODUCTION

Occupational licensing laws are not enforced the same way as most other laws. State regulatory boards, armed with rulemaking and enforcement authority, are the entities usually responsible for administering occupational licensing laws. Boards often use this power—delegated to them by state legislatures—to impose unjustifiable and anticompetitive burdens on the markets they regulate, frequently with little or no accountability.

For example, in 2020, the Texas dental board issued guidance for dental practices during the COVID-19 pandemic. Buried within this guidance was a declaration that "dentists in Texas are not authorized to practice teledentistry" because "Texas currently does not have rules that would permit teledentistry." There was no statute or rule banning teledentistry or any statute authorizing the board to ban teledentistry. But the board interpreted its own rule for documenting the findings of tactile examinations to require a tactile examination at every visit—thereby imposing a de facto ban on remote examinations. This was not a reasonable or necessary interpretation of the regulation. The board's decision eliminated access to dental care for many rural families and prevented Texans from seeking remote dental healthcare assistance while offices were closed in the

* Joshua Polk is Attorney at Pacific Legal Foundation. Stephen Slivinski is a senior fellow at the Cato Institute. Caleb Trotter is Attorney at Pacific Legal Foundation.

early days of the pandemic. While getting rid of teledentistry didn't help patients, it was a boon for brick-and-mortar dental offices who no longer had to compete against teledentistry services. After Pacific Legal Foundation filed a lawsuit challenging the board's anticompetitive decree, the state legislature responded by prohibiting the board from banning teledentistry in the state. In this case, the state stepped in to correct a rogue agency's anticompetitive actions, but most boards go unchallenged.[1]

There is a simple explanation for anticompetitive agency behavior: state regulatory boards are often staffed and controlled by interested parties that benefit financially from raising arbitrary barriers to new competition. For example, in Texas, 9 of the 11 dental board members were practicing members of the dental industry who would directly benefit from additional barriers to entry for prospective services. Using this state-granted privilege and power, board members who are themselves market participants can deny opportunities to prospective entrepreneurs by raising anticompetitive barriers to entry or exercising enforcement authority to quash innovation and competition. Simply put, cartels of existing businesses and market incumbents use regulatory authority to protect themselves against competition from newcomers or practitioners in a related field.

This reality is confirmed by research that shows overbearing regulatory actions arise not as a plea from the public or out of a concern for public health, but out of the interests of the regulated parties themselves. Board member market participants understand that the high cost of complying with regulatory burdens makes it more difficult to enter an occupation or innovate within it.

To date, however, legal challenges to state boards' anticompetitive and overbearing behavior have produced largely disappointing results. When litigants challenge anticompetitive occupational restrictions, courts most often apply the so-called rational basis

1. *Meadows v. Odom*, 360 F. Supp. 2d 811, 825 (M.D. La. 2005), offers a tragic example of the way that licensees exploit regulatory power for personal gain. There, Leslie Meadows challenged the constitutionality of a Louisiana law that required prospective florists to undergo a subjective two-part written and practical exam to obtain a florist license. *Id.* at 823. The exams were judged by practicing members of the industry. Ms. Meadows presented evidence that the state adopted the law solely to protect established florists against competition, excluding people from entry-level flower-arranging jobs that might have allowed them to provide for themselves and their families. Ms. Meadows lost her job as a result of the licensing requirement. Lacking the education and resources to find other employment, she died in poverty shortly after the court rejected her due process challenge. *See* Timothy Sandefur, *Insiders, Outsiders, and the American Dream: How Certificate of Necessity Laws Harm Our Society's Values*, 26 NOTRE DAME J.L. ETHICS & PUB. POL'Y 381, 401–03 (2012); and Caleb R. Trotter, *Exhuming the Privileges or Immunities Clause to Bury Rational-Basis Review*, 60 LOYOLA L. REV. 909, 910–12 (2014).

test. Under this test—one reserved for rights supposedly considered "non-fundamental" by the Supreme Court—courts will uphold regulations or allow government activity that "rationally serves a legitimate government interest." In practice, this test typically amounts to nothing more than a judicial rubber stamp and rarely results in a victory against the government. Thus, traditional Fourteenth Amendment claims—such as equal protection and due process—against anticompetitive economic regulations have proved difficult to win, and nearly impossible in some federal judicial circuits. New strategies must be developed to protect freedom from overbearing economic regulation.

This paper suggests one such legal and legislative strategy: using federal antitrust law and policy arguments about the fundamentally anticompetitive nature of licensing boards to restrict their ability to excessively burden entrepreneurs and hinder competition.

I. THE SCOPE OF THE PROBLEM

State regulatory boards, armed with rulemaking and enforcement authority, regularly impose unjustifiable, anticompetitive burdens on the markets they regulate. The growth of occupational licensure in recent years illustrates the impact that state regulatory bodies have on a wide variety of markets. In the 1950s, only 5 percent of occupations required a license, while today, the number has risen to nearly 33 percent.[2] State agencies regularly impose burdensome licensing requirements and regulations on innocuous occupations such as interior design or funeral directing in addition to fields implicating public health or safety such as medicine or law. In many cases, state regulatory boards have been slowly expanding the scope of their own authority to apply to activities outside the regulated field's traditional practices. This is known as licensure creep.

As the former chairperson of the Federal Trade Commission (FTC) Maureen Ohlhausen has remarked, there is no public safety rationale for expanding industry barriers to entry in this way.[3] The reality is that state regulatory boards are systematically staffed and controlled by interested parties that benefit from raising arbitrary barriers to new

---

2. Dick M. Carpenter II, et al., *License to Work: A National Study of Burdens from Occupational Licensing* 6, Institute for Justice (2012).

3. *See* Maureen K. Ohlhausen, *Advancing Economic Liberty*, George Mason Law Review's 20th Annual Antitrust Symposium (Feb. 23, 2017) ("I challenge anyone to explain why the state has a legitimate interest in protecting the public from rogue interior designers carpet-bombing living rooms with ugly throw pillows.").

competition. With this state-granted privilege, board members who are also market participants can deny opportunities to prospective entrepreneurs by raising anticompetitive barriers to entry or exercising enforcement authority to quash innovation and competition.[4] Cartels of existing businesses and market incumbents use regulatory authority to protect themselves against competition by newcomers or by practitioners in a related field.[5] By staffing regulatory agencies with established market participants who have a vested interest in excluding competition, states enable those firms to restrict entrepreneurs' practices, increase prices, and limit consumer choice.

A. Composition of Boards

There are nearly 1,800 occupational licensing boards in the United States. By the most recent available estimate, 85 percent of them are "required by statute to be comprised of a majority of currently licensed professionals, active in the very profession the board regulates."[6] Or, in other words, what the Supreme Court of the United States has termed "active market participants."[7]

Boards often include at least one nonlicensed member representing the public or consumers. State law may even require that this board member not have any "pecuniary interest" in the industry being regulated. Yet, those seats are a small minority in comparison. The average vote share of public members is usually below 30 percent of the board seats for any industry, meaning public members can be easily outvoted.[8] And

---

4. *See* Hallie v. City of Eau Claire, 471 U.S. 34, 47 (1985) ("Where a private party is engaging in the anticompetitive activity, there is a real danger that he is acting to further his own interests, rather than the governmental interests of the State.").

5. For example, in 2003, the FTC investigated anticompetitive conduct by dental boards when it charged the South Carolina Board of Dentistry with illegally preventing dental hygienists from providing basic preventative care to underprivileged children. Complaint at 1, In the Matter of South Carolina State Board of Dentistry (FTC 2003) (Docket No. 9311). Based on its concern that impoverished children were not receiving care, the South Carolina legislature had eliminated a law that required dentists to examine each child prior to a hygienist offering basic services. *Id.* at 3–4. But the nine-member dental board, comprised of seven licensed dentists and two public members, reinstated the policy. *Id.* at 5. The FTC concluded that the board's actions "deprived thousands of schoolchildren—particularly economically disadvantaged schoolchildren—of the benefits of preventative oral health care" without justification. *Id.* at 7.

6. Rebecca Haw Allensworth, *Foxes at the Henhouse: Licensing Boards Up Close*, 105 CAL. L. REV. 1567, 1570 (2017).

7. North Carolina St. Bd. of Dental Examiners v. FTC, 574 U.S. 494 (2015).

8. Authors' analysis based on data from Allensworth and updated by Pacific Legal Foundation.

that's assuming the public members have a vote on a matter before the board; many boards don't allow public members to vote on disciplinary or investigative actions or other board matters. Furthermore, many public seats go unfilled, allowing the active market participants to have complete de facto control over all significant board matters.

Powerless as many public board members are in the states where they exist, some states don't even bother with the window dressing of requiring public members on the board at all. For instance, seven states have no seats reserved for public members in statute for their cosmetology board.[9] Dental boards are 100 percent controlled by active market participants in four states.[10]

B. Appointment of Members

Members of state licensing boards are usually appointed by the governor or are nominated by the governor and then confirmed by the legislature. State law requires that members meet certain qualifications, such as having industry experience or holding an existing license in good standing.[11]

In some states, however, this process is also controlled largely by the active market participants that the board regulates. In those states, the governor may only choose board appointments from a list of candidates provided by the professional associations of the industries. Some statutes explicitly name which of these associations shall provide the lists, or they require that the lists contain only three or four names. In other cases, the professional association holds an election open only to existing licensees, and then the governor must rubber-stamp the winners.

A Pacific Legal Foundation research report published in 2022 looked at the nomination process for licensing boards across all 50 states for seventeen licensed professions. Among those, 23 states effectively hand over the power of nominating the private sector board members to a trade association for at least one board.[12]

9. See also LA. STAT. ANN. § 37:3173, which requires every member of the Louisiana interior design board to be a licensed interior designer with trade association membership.

10. Authors' analysis based on data from Allensworth and updated by Pacific Legal Foundation.

11. Some states impose further demographic restrictions requiring race- or sex-balanced boards in clear violation of the Constitution's guarantee of equal protection. Laura D'Agostino and Angela C. Erickson, *Public Service Denied*, Pacific Legal Foundation (2023).

12. Stephen Slivinski, *Choosing the Gatekeepers: How Special Interests Control Licensing Board Nominations*, Pacific Legal Foundation (Oct. 2022), https://pacificlegal.org/licensing-board-nominations-gatekeepers/.

The states with the largest number of occupations regulated by boards on which the private sector members are recommended by a trade association are Louisiana (12 occupations), Alabama (11 occupations), Mississippi (10 occupations), Kentucky (9 occupations), Oklahoma (8 occupations), Maryland (8 occupations), and North Carolina (8 occupations). Trade associations most frequently direct the selection of private sector board members for podiatrists (10 states), accountants (9 states), psychologists (9 states), dentists (8 states), nurses (8 states), and optometrists (8 states).[13]

These statistics demonstrate the monumental scale at which the states have transferred regulatory authority from themselves to private actors personally interested in raising additional barriers to entry. However, this has rendered the anticompetitive behaviors by many of these boards vulnerable to legal and legislative attack.

C. *N.C. Dental*: Antitrust Law's Pro-Liberty Application

The Sherman Act prohibits combinations and agreements that "unreasonably restrain trade." Ordinarily, this antitrust prohibition has been used to target private companies and individuals that allegedly collaborate to avoid competition. However, after the Supreme Court's decision in *N.C. Dental*,[14] there is at least one application of antitrust law that reaches the greatest perpetrators of anticompetitive activity—captured regulatory boards. At the time the Supreme Court issued its opinion, the North Carolina Board of Dental Examiners was a statutorily created agency composed of six dentists—selected by other licensed dentists—and two nondentist members. It was responsible for enforcing regulations regarding the scope of the practice of dentistry. When nondentists began offering teeth-whitening services to consumers, the board began sending cease-and-desist letters to these nondentists and threatening them with various penalties, some of them criminal. The board insisted that the only legal way to whiten teeth was by earning a dental license, which would require at least a dental degree from an accredited institution along with satisfying other regulatory requirements.

The FTC filed a complaint against the board, charging it with engaging in unfair practices through its market participant members. The board claimed immunity from federal

13. Ibid.
14. 574 U.S. 494 (2015).

antitrust law, and an appeal on that issue eventually reached the Supreme Court. In 2015, the Court reprimanded the board and, by extension, similarly dominated boards—what the legal and economic literature refer to as "captured" boards. Ordinarily, states are exempt from antitrust law under *Parker v. Brown*.[15] But here, the Court held that boards dominated by "active market participants" that engage in anticompetitive behavior could not claim an exemption from antitrust liability. The Court recognized the conflict of interest maintained by board members actively participating in the market they are simultaneously regulating. This reasoning was consistent with other antitrust precedent recognizing the danger of placing control over an industry into the hands of interested private parties. As Justice Burger had observed decades before, if antitrust policy was "meant to deal comprehensively and effectively with the evils resulting from contracts, combinations and conspiracies in restraint of trade," then it is "wholly arbitrary" to treat government-imposed restraints of trade as "beyond the purview of federal law."[16]

The widely stated goal of supporters of antitrust laws—that is, protection of the public—must be considered in light of not just economic realities but also the institutional realities of government. As Justice Stevens wrote in 1978, "In our complex economy the number of items that may cause serious harm is almost endless. . . . The judiciary cannot indirectly protect the public against this harm by conferring monopoly privileges on the manufacturers."[17]

II. LITIGATING ECONOMIC LIBERTY AFTER *N.C. DENTAL*

Relying on Fourteenth Amendment legal theories meriting only rational basis review has been an inconsistent and often failing method to defend economic liberty in the courts. When it is available, litigators should consider attacking anticompetitive government behavior through federal antitrust law. Antitrust challenges benefit from a higher standard of review ("rule of reason" rather than the highly deferential rational basis

15. 317 U.S. 341, 350 (1943).

16. City of Lafayette, La. v. Louisiana Power & Light Co., 435 U.S. 389, 419 (1978).

17. National Society of Professional Engineers v. U.S., 435 U.S. 679, 98 S. Ct. 1355, 55 L.Ed.2d 637 (1978).

standard) and courts are often skeptical of interested private parties with regulatory authority.[18]

Federal antitrust policy prohibits combinations and agreements that "unreasonably restrain trade."[19] Unfortunately, the storied history of Sherman Act enforcement is rife with conflicting judicial precedents, interminably shifting standards, and the stamping out of competitive market behavior (e.g., mergers, price decreases, vertical market integration, etc.). Contrary to its designers' stated purpose, antitrust policy has been a disaster for free market principles and economic liberty.[20] On the other hand, it has been a boon for lethargic companies which are insulated from innovative competition by antitrust enforcement.[21]

Antitrust legislation is under no serious threat of either repeal or of being declared unconstitutional by the judiciary. The Supreme Court has declared the Sherman Act the "Magna Carta of free enterprise," suggesting that "antitrust laws in general . . . are as important to the preservation of economic freedom . . . as the Bill of Rights is to the protection of . . . fundamental personal freedoms."[22] Further, antitrust regulatory authorities systematically punish companies for competitive innovation at the behest of market participants uneager or unable to compete absent government intervention.[23]

But despite the many shortcomings of antitrust enforcement, federal antitrust policy may be used as a tool to challenge anticompetitive state regulatory boards captured by market participants. As laid out above, the Supreme Court has applied the Sherman Act's prohibition on agreements that unreasonably restrain trade against state regulatory

---

18. Hoover v. Ronwin, 466 U.S. 558, 584 (1984) (Stevens, J., dissenting) (recognizing that empowering private parties to exploit licensing laws allows them "to advance their own interests in restraining competition at the expense of the public interest").

19. 15 U.S.C. § 1 (Sherman Act).

20. See generally Dominick T. Armentano, Antitrust and Monopoly: Anatomy of a Policy Failure (Independent Institute 2d ed., 1999).

21. ROBERT BORK, THE ANTITRUST PARADOX 137–67 (2021 ed.).

22. U.S. v. Topco Associates, Inc., 405 U.S. 596, 610 (1972).

23. FTC Seeks to Block Microsoft Corp.'s Acquisition of Activision Blizzard, Inc., FEDERAL TRADE COMMISSION (Dec. 8, 2022), https://www.ftc.gov/news-events/news/press-releases/2022/12/ftc-seeks -block-microsoft-corps-acquisition-activision-blizzard-inc.

boards acting on behalf of private interests.[24] States acting as sovereigns and imposing state policy are exempt from antitrust liability—also known as "*Parker* immunity."[25] However, this exemption is disfavored when claimed by state boards dominated by private market interests.[26] A state regulatory board controlled by market participants is entitled to state-action immunity only if (1) the challenged anticompetitive policy is clearly articulated by state statute; and (2) enforcement of the anticompetitive policy is actively supervised by the state.[27] Thus, for purposes of bringing antitrust challenges to state board activity, it is important to strategically select boards particularly vulnerable under the *Midcal* standard. The small number of antitrust cases filed against government regulatory boards after *N.C. Dental* illustrate some of the difficulties in developing such a case. The first difficulty is identifying boards vulnerable to antitrust scrutiny. The following sections discuss which boards are suitable targets for litigation.

A. Boards Dominated by Market Participants

Under *N.C. Dental*, for a state regulatory board to be subject to antitrust liability, it must be dominated by market participants. The critical threshold question is then whether market participants exercise control over the board's anticompetitive activities.[28] The Supreme Court has never articulated a clear-cut standard for what constitutes domination by market participants. And there is no significant case law creating specific guidelines on this issue. However, the Court made clear in *N.C. Dental* that a state board on which a *controlling* (not necessarily a majority) number of decisionmakers are active market participants must satisfy the *Midcal* standard to claim immunity from antitrust enforcement. Absent a clear majority, whether market participants control a particular board depends on factual context. There are at least

24. *N.C. Dental*, 574 U.S. at 505.

25. *See Parker*, 317 U.S. at 350.

26. *See* FTC. v. Phoebe Putney Health System, Inc., 568 U.S. 216 (2013).

27. *See* California Retail Liquor Dealers Assn. v. Midcal Aluminum, Inc., 445 U.S. 97, 105 (1980).

28. There is another threshold question of whether a board's anticompetitive behavior affects interstate commerce. There are two ways to answer this question: (1) the "flow of commerce test" which considers whether the challenged activity acts directly upon or within the stream of interstate commerce and (2) the "substantial effects" test which allows federal antitrust scrutiny of intrastate conduct if it has a "substantial effect" on activities within interstate commerce. *Goldfarb v. Virginia St. Bar*, 421 U.S. 773, 784 n.11 (1975); *see Hospital Bldg. Co. v. Trustees of Rex Hospital*, 425 U.S. 738, 743 (1976).

two circumstances outside of a basic majority in which a board might be deemed to be dominated by market participants: (1) if market participants have veto power over board decisions; or (2) if market participants can meet and decide certain issues without non–market participant members' approval. The specifics of a particular case might also reveal that market participants have an outsized influence over enforcement or rulemaking decisions.

There are studies that reveal the level of capture experienced by regulatory boards in a wide variety of fields. Available research, discussed above, shows the number of industry insiders currently placed on regulatory boards in several states across several fields. The higher the number of market participants on any particular board, the more likely a challenge to the board will satisfy the threshold question of market domination. However, a board should not be ignored as a potential antitrust target solely because fewer than a majority of decisionmakers are market participants. For purposes of resource conservation, the most captured boards likely make the best targets—and are also the most likely to erect anticompetitive barriers or quash innovative approaches through regulatory enforcement.

B. Clear Articulation

As is often the case in the context of federal antitrust policy, the Supreme Court has not provided a clear-cut standard for whether a government body's anticompetitive policy is "clearly articulated" by state statute and thus immune from antitrust liability. However, the Supreme Court has clarified the standard and corrected lower courts' overreliance on an overly generous "foreseeability" standard.[29] Prior to the Court's ruling, lower courts had applied a loose standard under which so long as anticompetitive behavior was foreseeable from a state's grant of authority, the anticompetitive policy was "clearly articulated." Similar to the rational basis test, this standard often proved to be nothing more than a judicial rubber stamp in practice. However, in *Phoebe Putney*, the Supreme Court made clear that "clear articulation" required much more. Rather, it identified several requirements for "clear articulation" in addition to basic foreseeability, including the following:

---

29. *See* FTC v. Phoebe Putney Health Sys., 568 U.S. 216 (2013).

1. The anticompetitive behavior must be the "inherent, logical, or ordinary result" of the state policy.

2. State statutory authority to act in general is not sufficient; rather, the challenged government body must show it was delegated the authority to act or regulate anticompetitively.

3. There must be evidence that the state affirmatively contemplated that the scheme would displace competition.

4. Where a state's position is one of mere neutrality to competition, the state cannot be said to have contemplated anticompetitive conduct.

5. Simple permission to operate in the market is not the authority to act anticompetitively.

6. Authorization of specific forms of anticompetitive conduct, like a certificate of need program, does not establish that the state affirmatively contemplated other forms of anticompetitive conduct.

7. Federalism concerns do not require the Court to err in favor of finding immunity— once again setting the standard apart from the rational basis test

As discussed above, boards often push the limits of any legitimate authority they have been granted by statute. Licensure creep, unsupervised cease and desist campaigns, and other anticompetitive behaviors are often performed outside the scope of statutory authority. To identify boards vulnerable to antitrust liability under this prong of the *Midcal* test, close examination of the text of a statutory delegation of authority will be necessary. If the statute fails to clearly articulate an anticompetitive policy later adopted by the regulatory board, the board will not be entitled to immunity from antitrust liability.

C. Active Supervision

Similar to the "clear articulation" standard, whether a board's anticompetitive behavior is actively supervised by the state depends on the facts of a particular case. There isn't a large body of law providing guidance on this standard, but the Supreme Court has made clear that this, like "clear articulation," is not a "rubber stamp" requirement. Rather, supervision must be real and it must precede implementation of the allegedly anticompetitive behavior. In other words, subsequent judicial or administrative review is not sufficient to confer immunity on a captured board. In *N.C. Dental*, the Court articulated basic components of active supervision:

1. The state supervisor must review the substance of the anticompetitive action, not merely the procedures followed to produce it.
2. The state supervisor must have the power to veto or modify particular decisions in accordance with state policy.
3. Potential for state supervision is not an adequate substitute for an actual decision by the state.
4. The state supervisor must not be a market participant.

It also made clear the sorts of state supervision that do *not* satisfy the "active supervision" requirement, including

1. Cursory or nonsubstantive review of the board's conduct
2. General, ongoing advice to the board
3. A "supervisor" who has no authority to disapprove anticompetitive acts

For potential litigation, it's important to identify boards that are not being actively supervised by the state. Research into the statutory grant of authority, and the boards' regulations themselves will likely uncover whether there is a supervision apparatus in place for a board's anticompetitive behavior.

D. Antitrust Merits

Defeating immunity is only the first step in a successful antitrust claim against captured regulatory boards. On the merits of the claim, one must show that there was an explicit or tacit agreement to unreasonably restrain trade.[30] Evidence must show that the restraint of trade was an agreement between separate economic actors pursuing separate economic interests, such that the agreement "deprives the marketplace of independent centers of decision making."[31]

It's rare for colluding market participants to announce their anticompetitive agreements; thus, in most cases, direct or circumstantial evidence must suggest the existence

---

30. Standard Oil Co. v. United States, 221 U.S. 1, 59–60 (1911).

31. *See* American Needle, Inc. v. Nat'l Football League, 560 U.S. 183, 195 (2010).

of an agreement. For case selection strategy, it is important to identify consistent patterns of anticompetitive behavior by market participant board members. For example, if a board engages in an unsupervised campaign of sending cease and desist letters to would-be competitors, the circumstantial evidence could suggest the existence of agreement between board members to shut down competition.[32] Where there is an agreement to restrain trade, one must also show that there is an impact on competition—not just on a particular market participant.[33] It may be difficult to prove an impact on market competition absent a pattern of anticompetitive behavior.[34] However, unauthorized single actions, like the Texas dental board banning teledentistry in 2020, *can* unreasonably burden competition in violation of federal antitrust law. Boards might also chill competitive innovation through enforcement actions against those offering services apparently outside the scope of the regulated field (e.g., the teeth whiteners targeted in *N.C. Dental*).

It is important to note that antitrust actions of this nature will not directly result in the elimination of burdensome licensing statutes. However, a victory on antitrust grounds would remove power from interested decisionmakers and undermine the legitimacy of anticompetitive board behavior. It may also spur statutory reform, like in Texas, stripping power from captured boards and generating closer state supervision. Finally, if issued by a board untethered to clear statutory authority, an antitrust lawsuit could result in the termination of anticompetitive licensing requirements that would improve economic opportunity.

III. LEGISLATIVE REMEDIES TO REFORM ANTI-COMPETITIVE BOARDS

In the context of occupational licensing in particular, there is another strategy that doesn't seek to directly strike down the laws that hinder economic liberty but instead to take aim at the structures that perpetuate and extend those violations of economic liberty. A strategy complementing litigation would be statutory reform of occupational licensing

---

32. *See N.C. Dental.*

33. National Soc'y of Prf'l Eng'rs v. United States, 435 U.S. 679, 690 (1978).

34. *C.f.* Oksanen v. Page Mem'l Hosp., 945 F.2d 696 (4th Cir. 1991) (holding that it did not unreasonably burden competition to suspend the license of one electrician for allegedly substandard work).

boards, using the guidance of *N.C. Dental*. The reforms below would be aimed at either clarifying or reducing board power, increasing public input on board decisions, or both. Statutory reforms like these have the potential to be more durable than litigation victories as well as broader and more immediate. However, none of them alone are a silver bullet, and any effective reform would include at least two of the elements, and preferably all of them.

A. Stricter and Clearer Definitions of Board Power

A key element of the *N.C. Dental* case was whether the dental board actually had the power to act as they did. Enforcement powers that boards assume they have in many states stem from a self-serving and expansive interpretation of sometimes opaque or unclear statutes that delegate enforcement powers to the board. One way of remedying this problem is to be as explicit as possible about what powers the boards do and do not have. It would be incumbent upon legislators, however, to refine this list of powers so as not to violate other requirements pertaining to the traditional delegation of government powers. This could, and in many cases should, necessitate reducing the actual powers the boards have in many states.

B. Requirement of Active Supervision of Boards

The *N.C. Dental* decision touched on the question of whether the North Carolina board was actively supervised by the state, although it didn't provide substantial guidance on what constitutes such supervision. It was obvious, however, that passive supervision, such as occasional review by the attorney general's office or sporadic oversight by the state legislature, would not pass muster. Yet, putting into state statute a requirement that some agency within government (executive or legislative) periodically review the decisions and actions of the board could bring a state closer in compliance to Supreme Court precedent.

Another way to create an institutional form of active supervision by the executive branch would be to fold a licensing board into an existing executive branch agency, such as a medical board being moved into the state department of health or a board of contractors being moved under a bureau of licensing. The assumption here is that a board would only be able to do what the agency would allow it to do, since it is now effectively part of the agency. Indeed, the licensing board could be modified to be an advisory board only to the executive agency's head. Requiring an agency head to sign off on any decisions reached by the board would provide further supervision and accountability to boards that might otherwise be prone to going rogue.

C. Increase the Number of the Non–Market Participant Seats on the Board

Increased public input to board decisions might help minimize excessive enforcement activities by the board and provide a check to cartel-like activity. Additionally, adding voting seats to be filled by representatives of an executive branch agency might also potentially satisfy the need for active executive supervision. Creating parity between public or executive branch seats and licensee seats is a worthwhile goal. (Indeed, giving nonlicensees a majority of the board seats—which is the case in some states for some occupations in some states—should also be considered.)[35] Vesting the holders of those board seats with voting rights on all board decisions would also be important in any of these scenarios.

D. Restore Power to the Governor to Appoint Board Members

Affirming the governor's prerogative to select whomever they deem best to serve on the board—provided those nominees fit the other criteria in statute—would restore accountability to the board nomination process and, presumably, to board actions. Statutes could still allow trade associations to recommend names, but governors should not be required to appoint from that list. In other words, governors would have the power to appoint licensing board members just as they do other board members and agency heads in other areas of government—and, in doing so, provide the standard accountability and transparency that comes with that more traditional appointment process.

---

35. After years of aggressive and arbitrary actions by the state cosmetology board—a high-profile example being an investigation of a volunteer giving free haircuts to homeless veterans in public parks in Tucson—Arizona recently enacted a change to their cosmetology board statutes that increased the number of public members defined as those "who are not and have never been associated with the barbering, cosmetology or nail technology industry, licensed as a barber, cosmetologist or nail technician or involved in manufacturing barbering, cosmetology or nail technology products" to a majority (five seats out of eight). *See* AZ REV. STAT. § 32–502 (2022).

E. Eliminate Licensing Boards

The best solution is to eliminate licensing boards altogether. That does not require eliminating the license requirements themselves, although that would also be preferable. What it does mean is that the license is issued and enforced by a specific executive branch agency, presided over by an appointed agency head. Licensing boards as they exist now could instead be formulated to serve as advisory councils with no power of enforcement or veto of the agency head. This would not only clearly place the state within compliance of *N.C. Dental* but also create greater accountability of those who enforce and issue licenses. It would also largely eliminate the issues of licensing board capture that have been outlined here.

Navigating the Economic Liberty Jurisprudence: Lessons from Indian Legal Battles

By Prashant Narang*

INTRODUCTION

I n rule of law societies, the judiciary's primary role is to safeguard constitutional rights, acting as an eternal watchdog. Among these rights in India, freedom to pursue any livelihood is pivotal. Article 19(1)(g) of the Indian Constitution guarantees individuals the autonomy to engage in a profession, occupation, trade, or business. This freedom is fundamental for fostering entrepreneurship and innovation, thereby contributing to human flourishing. One might think that the judiciary's effectiveness in upholding these rights depends upon its procedural integrity and foundational independence, since the legal system's fairness and impartiality cultivates legitimacy and institutional credibility. It also depends on the judiciary's appreciation for the theoretical foundations of economic liberty, including first principles of wealth creation as well as the theory of common good that underpin the balance between individual freedoms and collective welfare.

Historical trajectory indicates the Supreme Court's evolutionary journey from a textualist approach to a more end-oriented eclecticism, marked by the Court's deference to state and public authorities.[1] Scholars affirm that the role of a constitutional court as

* Prashant Narang is a postdoctoral researcher at the Knee Regulatory Research Center at West Virginia University.
1. Chintan Chandrachud, *Constitutional Interpretation* in THE OXFORD HANDBOOK OF THE INDIAN CONSTITUTION (Sujit Choudhry, Madhav Khosla, & Pratap Bhanu Mehta eds., 2016).

the liberty sentinel is often fraught with challenges including political pressures and majoritarian expectations, thereby limiting the courts' ability in enforcing constitutional rights.[2] Further, potential conflicts of interest arising from postretirement job prospects for Supreme Court judges in India influence the neutrality of judicial decisionmaking in politically salient cases.[3] The Supreme Court of India is known for its polyvocality, reflecting an inconsistency and incoherence in decisions; varied bench compositions and a tendency toward small benches handling significant constitutional cases dilutes the quality of judicial reasoning in protecting freedoms.[4]

As far as economic freedom is concerned, the protection for reasonableness ground has significantly weakened as an evident lack of a coherent theoretical framework guiding judicial discretion in these matters leaves room for judicial whims.[5] And general public interest, which is the other ground for justifying an economic restriction enumerated under Article 19(6), has been insufficiently scrutinized.[6] Often bypassing thorough scrutiny in favor of deference, the Court favors state interests.[7]

Despite these studies, the literature reveals critical gaps in understanding the Supreme Court's approach to economic liberty. The scarcity of research into judicial ideology signals an overlooked dimension that could reveal profound insights into the decisionmaking process regarding economic liberties.[8] There is a critical need for a deeper engagement with Article 19(1)(g) jurisprudence and the influence of ideology and external factors on judicial behavior, in addition to the development of a robust theoretical framework to better understand and navigate the protection of economic freedoms within India's unique constitutional context.

2. Adam S. Chilton & Mila Versteeg, *Courts' Limited Ability to Protect Constitutional Rights*, 85 UNIV. CHIC. L. REV. 293 (2018).

3. Aney, et al., *Jobs for Justice(s): Corruption in the Supreme Court of India*, J. L. & ECON. (2021).

4. *Supra* note 1.

5. Vikramaditya Khanna, *Profession, Occupation, Trade or Business* in THE OXFORD HANDBOOK OF THE INDIAN CONSTITUTION, *supra* note 1.

6. Sukarm Sharma, *Rescuing Article 19 from the Golden Triangle*, 3–4 NUJS L. REV. (2022).

7. Prashant Narang, *Difficulty of Doing Business—A Study of Judicial Review of Economic Restrictions*, ADMINISTRATIVE LAW IN THE COMMON LAW WORLD (Jul. 17, 2018), https://adminlawblogorg.wordpress.com /2018/07/17/prashant-narang-difficulty-of-doing-business-a-study-of-judicial-review-of-economic -restrictions/.

8. Sunita Parikh, *Empirical Studies of Judicial Behaviour and Decision-Making on Indian Courts*, in HIGH COURTS IN GLOBAL PERSPECTIVE (Nuno Garoupa, Rebecca D. Gill, & Lydia B. Tiede eds., 2021).

To address this gap, the paper employs a qualitative methodology to explore the Supreme Court of India's judgments on economic restrictions under Article 19(1)(g). Specifically, it focuses on the influence of third-party interests. Employing operational definitions and a detailed analytical framework, it examines judicial reasoning, degree of scrutiny, and engagement with third-party interests. Through a systematic search and analysis of relevant cases, it discerns trends in the adjudication of constitutional challenges to economic restrictions with significant involvement of third-party rights.

The study argues that the Supreme Court tends to prioritize third-party interests in constitutional challenges to economic restrictions. In most cases, it does so without doing due scrutiny of economic restrictions, or it simply presumes the constitutionality of an economic restriction if it furthers a directive principle. The presence of a third-party interest, particularly a labor, consumer, or environmental interest, trumps business interests where these interests are not aligned. However, in cases where these interests are aligned, the outcomes are also favorable to business and professionals.

What implications does this study have for practitioners? It highlights the urgent need for pivoting litigation strategies for effectively navigating the constitutional adjudication involving economic liberties in tussle with third-party interests. It suggests that integrating and aligning third-party interests, such as those of labor and consumers, within legal arguments could markedly influence judicial outcomes in favor of economic freedoms. This framework should not only underscore the relevance of economic theories and the broader impact of entrepreneurship but also stress the need for a judicial approach that is both proportionate and grounded in public interest. By emphasizing the strategic integration of third-party interests into legal arguments, this paper seeks to offer a fresh perspective to the discourse on economic liberties in India, advocating for a methodological shift toward more informed and efficacious advocacy in constitutional litigation.

I. THE SUPREME COURT OF INDIA AND ECONOMIC LIBERTIES UNDER ARTICLE 19(1)(G): A DETAILED EXPLORATION

The judiciary's role in upholding constitutional rights within a society underscores the delicate balance between individual freedoms and state interests. This balance is particularly pertinent in the context of economic liberties, which are fundamental to a thriving democracy and market economy. In India, these liberties are enshrined in

Article 19(1)(g) of the Constitution, which guarantees citizens the right to practice any profession, or to carry on any occupation, trade, or business. However, the enforcement and protection of these rights by the judiciary, notably the Supreme Court of India, reveal a complex interplay of factors that challenge the efficacy of judicial oversight.

A. Historical and Legal Context

Initially, the Supreme Court of India adopted a textualist approach, focusing on the literal interpretation of the Constitution. Over time, this evolved into a more structuralist stance, considering the broader constitutional structure, and eventually led to what has been described as "panchayati eclecticism"—a term denoting a blend of various interpretative methods, leading to outcome-oriented decisions. This evolution reflects the Court's shifting philosophy toward a more pragmatic adjudication, albeit with significant implications for the consistency and coherence of its rulings.

Chilton and Versteeg (2018) articulate the multifaceted challenges courts face, such as the repercussions from political branches, strategic conflict avoidance, alignment with majoritarian preferences, and limitations in addressing rights violations like torture and social rights. These factors collectively contribute to the judiciary's nuanced struggle in safeguarding constitutional rights, including economic liberties.

B. Judicial Deference and Economic Regulation

A defining feature of the Supreme Court's approach to economic liberties under Article 19(1)(g) is its deference to state evaluations regarding restrictions on these fundamental rights. Despite extensive debate on the interpretation of terms like "reasonable" and "procedure established by law," the judiciary has often sided with the state. This trend indicates a broader pattern of judicial deference in matters of economic regulation, potentially influenced by postretirement incentives for judges, suggesting a conflict of interest that may sway judicial decisions in favor of the government.

C. Constitutional Provisions and Interpretations

Article 19(1)(g) represents a crucial aspect of economic liberty, allowing citizens the autonomy to engage in various economic activities. However, Article 19(6) introduces a caveat permitting the state to impose "reasonable restrictions" in the interest of the general public. This provision, while designed to balance individual freedoms with public welfare, lacks a precise definition of "public interest," leading to interpretative challenges.

The Indian Constitution, post amendments embracing socialism and downgrading the right to property, presents a unique blend of ideologies. It neither aligns strictly with capitalist principles nor adopts a fully socialist stance. The inclusion of the Ninth Schedule and the provisions allowing state monopolization further complicates the judiciary's task in adjudicating economic liberties. These constitutional complexities underscore the challenges in protecting economic freedoms while accommodating state policy objectives.

D. Scholarly Debate and Judicial Reasonableness

To what extent does the Supreme Court adhere to standards of review? There is a tendency for the judiciary to forego comprehensive review, opting instead for a deferential or partially scrutinized stance.[9] The judiciary narrowly focuses on reasonableness at the expense of "in the interest of general public"—a specific ground for restriction enumerated under Article 19(6).[10] This judicial reluctance to challenge state action raises concerns about the robustness of economic liberties' protection. Although the judiciary has curtailed state discretion, it has led to enhanced judicial discretion.[11] This shift, absent a sound theoretical framework, has replaced one form of arbitrariness with another.[12]

E. The Role of Judicial Ideology

Parikh underscores the scarcity of research into judicial ideology, especially at the Supreme Court level.[13] Understanding the ideological leanings of Justices could offer invaluable insights into the Court's decisionmaking process and its approach to economic liberties. This gap in the literature points to an unexplored avenue for examining how

9. *Supra* note 7.

10. *Supra* note 6.

11. INDIA CONST. art. 19, § 6.

12. *Supra* note 5.

13. *Supra* note 8.

individual and collective ideologies influence judicial behavior and case outcomes concerning economic freedoms.

F. Addressing Literature Gaps

Despite the wealth of scholarly attention to the judiciary's deferential stance and the various influences on judicial decisionmaking, a significant void exists in comprehensively understanding what factors lead judges to favor petitioner outcomes in cases involving economic liberties. This gap is critical, given the paramount importance of such liberties in fostering entrepreneurship, innovation, and individual livelihoods—essential components of a thriving democratic and market-oriented society.

The Court's frequent deference, coupled with neglect of grounds of review and infrequency of pro-petitioner decisions in the domain of economic liberties, necessitates a closer examination of the judiciary's inclination and preferences. Identifying the conditions under which the judiciary is more inclined to uphold individual economic freedoms over state interests is crucial for developing strategies to strengthen the protection of these rights.

G. Conclusion

This detailed exploration into the Supreme Court of India's engagement with Article 19(1)(g) reveals the intricate challenges and considerations involved in upholding economic liberties. The historical evolution of the Court's jurisprudence, the constitutional framework governing economic rights, and the scholarly debate surrounding judicial deference and reasonableness collectively paint a complex picture of the judicial landscape in India. By identifying key gaps in the literature, this review sets the stage for further research aimed at enhancing our understanding of judicial processes and developing robust legal frameworks to better advocate for economic liberties in the Indian context.

II. METHODOLOGY

This study examines the dynamics between economic restrictions, judicial decisionmaking, and third-party interests. Central to this inquiry is Article 19(1)(g) of the Indian Constitution, which guarantees the right to practice any profession, or to carry on any occupation, trade, or business, subject to reasonable restrictions in the interest of the general public. The aim is to systematically explore how third-party interests—either aligned or in conflict with those of the business—influence cases involving constitutional challenges to economic restrictions.

A. Operational Definitions

It is important to begin with clear operational definitions for the core concepts to provide a foundation for the analytical framework and also ensure uniformity in the interpretation and categorization of the collected data.

- Judicial review: This term refers to the in-depth examination undertaken by the Supreme Court to assess the constitutionality and justification of state-imposed restrictions on economic liberties. Such review scrutinizes the proportionality, reasonableness, and necessity of the restrictions in question, ensuring they are not arbitrary and they serve a legitimate public interest.
- Economic restrictions: Economic restrictions are any state-imposed limits or regulations on the right to practice any profession, or to carry on any occupation, trade, or business that are under challenge in the judgment. In the context of this study, economic restrictions specifically refer to those challenges under Article 19(1)(g) of the Constitution, focusing on their impact on business operations and the associated legal debates regarding their constitutionality.
- Third-party interests: Third-party interests include the rights or interests of individuals or groups other than the primary parties involved in a case—namely, the state and the business entity or professional challenging the restriction. These may include labor groups, consumers, environmental advocates, and other indirect beneficiaries or victims of economic regulations.
- Alignment and conflict of interests: These concepts refer to the relationship between the interests of business entities challenging economic restrictions and those of third parties. Alignment occurs when both parties' interests are either mutually beneficial or adversely affected by the restriction in question. Conflict arises when the restriction benefits one party at the expense of the other, creating a zero-sum situation. Understanding this dynamic is crucial for

analyzing how the presence and nature of third-party interests influence judicial decisions.

B. Data Collection Process

This section delineates the strategies employed to identify, filter, and compile relevant judgments for analysis.

Using Casemine, the search for relevant cases is conducted using a combination of keywords, Boolean operators, and specific filters. The primary keyword is "Article 19(1)(g)." Filters are applied to narrow down the search results to the Supreme Court and the timeframe from 2010 to 2024.

Cases that substantively engage with Article 19(1)(g), demonstrate a constitutional challenge to economic restrictions, and involve third-party interests are flagged for detailed analysis.

Selected cases are systematically documented and cataloged, with essential information such as case title, citation, date of judgment, issue, and judges.

Inclusion criteria:

- Engagement with Article 19(1)(g): This means the Court's examination of the case revolves significantly around the interpretation and application of Article 19(1)(g). The case must involve a challenge to state-imposed restrictions on economic liberties, whether in the form of legislation, administrative actions, or other legal instruments. These restrictions should directly impact the ability to practice any profession or to carry on any occupation, trade, or business.
- Involvement of third-party interests: Cases where either the judgment discusses the impact of restriction on a third party, or the restriction itself furthers a third-party interest are included. "Third-party interests" means the rights or interests of individuals or groups beyond the immediate parties (the state and the business entity) are at stake.
- Judicial review outcome: Cases are included where the Supreme Court has provided a clear decision or interpretation concerning the constitutionality and justification of the economic restrictions, considering the balance between individual rights and public interest.
- Dissenting opinion, if any, is included.

Exclusion criteria:

- Peripheral mention of Article 19(1)(g): Cases where Article 19(1)(g) is mentioned only in passing or as a peripheral issue without substantive judicial analysis are excluded.
- Constitutional amendments as the primary focus: Cases primarily challenging constitutional amendments, rather than specific economic restrictions under Article 19(1)(g), are excluded.
- Lack of direct economic restriction challenge: Cases filed for directions or involving public interest litigation that do not directly challenge an economic restriction affecting business operations are excluded. This criterion ensures the analysis remains tethered to the study's core concern with economic restrictions.
- Appeals against High Court directions: Appeals that do not involve any economic restrictions and involve either passing directions or reviewing High Court—passed directions are excluded.

The analytical framework consists of several categories designed to organize the data and facilitate a comprehensive analysis:

- Sector/type of economic activity challenged: Each case is categorized based on the specific business or profession subject to the economic restriction. This helps in understanding the scope and variety of economic activities impacted by judicial decisions and allows for the identification of patterns or trends within specific sectors.
- Issue at stake: The core issue challenged in the case, whether it pertains to the constitutionality of the restriction, its reasonableness, proportionality, or necessity, is identified. This allows for an exploration of the legal grounds on which economic restrictions are contested.
- Outcome of the case: Cases are analyzed based on their outcomes—whether the judgment was in favor of the state (upholding the restriction) or the individual/business (overturning the restriction). This provides insight into the judiciary's inclination toward economic freedom or regulatory interests.
- Presence and nature of third-party interests: This category examines whether third-party interests are present and identifies what these third-party interests are

(e.g., consumer, labor, environmental). Understanding the role and perspective of third parties enriches the analysis of judicial reasoning and outcomes.

- Impact on third-party interests: The outcome of the case for third-party interests is noted, including whether the decision was against or in favor of these interests. This assessment helps in gauging the judiciary's consideration of broader societal impacts beyond the immediate parties.
- Rights and principles invoked: The analysis looks at the fundamental rights or Directive Principles of State Policy (DPSP) invoked in favor of or against third-party interests.
- Relationship between business and third party: The alignment or conflict between business entities and third-party interests is assessed. Cases are analyzed to determine whether the impugned restriction adversely impacts both parties (A = Aligned) or benefits one at the expense of the other (N = Not aligned).

Limitations:

- Scope of data: The study is confined to judgments from the Supreme Court of India, focusing on Article 19(1)(g). While this provides a concentrated view of high-level jurisprudence, it may not capture the full spectrum of legal discourse on economic restrictions and third-party interests across different levels of the judiciary.
- Interpretative analysis: Given the qualitative nature of much of the analysis, interpretations of judicial reasoning and outcomes are subject to the researchers' perspectives.
- Dynamic legal landscape: The legal landscape, especially regarding economic regulations and rights, is continuously evolving. The study captures the state of jurisprudence from 2010 to 2024 only.

This methodology lays the groundwork for a focused study of the Supreme Court of India's handling of economic restrictions under Article 19(1)(g), emphasizing third-party interests. Utilizing a detailed analytical framework, it aims to dissect judgments to reveal how the Court balances business concerns with third-party rights. This approach promises a thorough inquiry, despite inherent limitations, striving to offer insights into the interplay between economic freedom and regulation. Ultimately, this research aspires to illuminate the effects of judicial decisions on economic policies and stakeholder interests, contributing to the scholarly dialogue on legal and economic governance and setting a precedent for further study in this crucial field.

III. FINDINGS

Thirteen judgments involved significant third-party interests.

Of the thirteen cases, nine feature nonaligned interests between businesses and third parties. Remarkably, in eight out of nine cases, the judgments favor the state and third-party interests, indicating a judicial tendency to prioritize public or third-party welfare over business interests when there is a conflict. Notably, one of these eight cases sparked a dissenting opinion that favors the business against third-party interests.[14] Out of these eight cases, three summarily rejected the claim without any review.[15] Three rejected the challenges based on the premise that a restriction in furtherance of a directive principle is presumed to be reasonable; all three cases referred to the relevant directive principles in detail.[16] The remaining two were related to state-conducted common admission tests for admission to private medical schools. The first one undertook a partial proportionality test while referring to precedents to justify the restrictions. The second one referred to this case and other precedents to uphold the common entrance exam.

Two cases were identified where business and third-party interests are aligned. The first case centers on the language of instruction in schools.[17] The Court affirmed parents' rights (and implicitly, those of educational businesses) to choose the medium of instruction by locating it in students' freedom of speech and expression.

The second case involves the prohibition of bar dancing, where the Court sided with the dignity and labor rights of women dancers against claims of obscenity, supporting

---

14. Society for Unaided Private Schools in Rajasthan v. Union of India (dissenting) (2012) 6 SCC 1.

15. Sharma Transports v. State of Maharashtra (2011) 8 SCC 647; ABP Private Ltd v. Union of India (2014) 3 SCC 327; Karnataka Live Band Restaurants Association v. State of Karnataka (2018) 4 SCC 372.

16. Society for Unaided Private Schools in Rajasthan v. Union of India (majority opinion) (2012) 6 SCC 1; Hindustan Zinc Limited v. Rajasthan Electricity Regulatory Commission (2015) 12 SCC 611; The Kerala Bar Hotels Associations v. State of Kerala, Civil Appeal no. 4417/2020.

17. State of Karnataka v. Associated Management of English Medium Primary and Secondary Schools (2014) 9 SCC 485.

both the businesses' operational freedoms and the workers' rights.[18] These decisions underscore the judiciary's receptiveness to aligned business and third-party interests, especially when fundamental rights and human dignity are at stake.

Two cases present mixed alignment of interests, complicating the narrative of alignment versus conflict. The first involves a challenge to mandatory iodization of salt, on grounds of consumer choice, access, and cost.[19] It was perceived to benefit large corporations at the expense of small traders—a situation where business interests are not clearly aligned or in conflict with third-party interests. As far as the economic liberty ground was concerned, the Court did not undertake a comprehensive review of the restriction; instead, it rejected the challenge summarily on grounds of deference. The Court viewed the restriction as a policy decision related to public health. Further, it observed that there was no material to show that a monopoly is sought to be created in favor of MNCs or large corporations. However, the Court invalidated the rule on the administrative law doctrine of *ultra vires*.

The second case, regarding licensing for bars and restaurants to permit dancing, reflects a balancing act where the Court modulates the regulatory framework to ensure the welfare of bar dancers while maintaining regulatory objectives.[20] This case illustrates the judiciary's attempt to navigate between upholding business operations and protecting third-party welfare.

This analysis reveals a nuanced judiciary stance toward balancing business operations, state regulations, and third-party interests. The predominance of cases favoring state and third-party interests over economic liberty in scenarios of conflict suggests a progressive inclination.

This refined analysis not only categorizes the cases based on the alignment of interests but also delves into the judicial rationale behind these categorizations, offering a deeper understanding of how certain interests are prioritized in the complex landscape of judicial review of economic restrictions.

18. State of Maharashtra v. Indian Hotels and Restaurants Association (2019) 3 SCC 429.

19. Academy of Nutrition Improvement v. Union of India (2011) 8 SCC 274.

20. Indian Hotel and Restaurant Association v. State of Maharashtra (2013) 8 SCC 519.

IV. DISCUSSION

A significant number of these rulings favor state restrictions and third-party interests over economic freedom, particularly in areas concerning morality, access to education, and environment. These judicial decisions, thus, underscore a pronounced commitment to addressing overarching majoritarian preferences. This commitment may serve as a mechanism to uphold the judiciary's legitimacy and public trust. Moreover, it suggests an acute judicial consciousness of the broader political and social ramifications of its rulings. Such a focus on credibility and legitimacy may inadvertently lead to a diminished adherence to the rigorous standards of review and the depth of justification traditionally anticipated in judicial assessments.

Echoing and expanding upon the observations made by Chilton and Versteeg (2018), this analysis reveals a judicial tendency to navigate cautiously within the realm of economic restrictions, wary of contradicting political authorities or straying from majoritarian preferences. This study elucidates a clear judicial inclination toward accommodating state and third-party interests, particularly when these clash with economic rights. This inclination toward caution may well be rooted in a strategic desire to preempt potential criticisms or restrictive actions from political entities, showcasing a judicious awareness of the judiciary's constrained role in the larger political landscape.

There is only one instance where members of the judiciary advocated against both the state and the third party in question to uphold the business interest. That isolated occurrence is a dissenting opinion. The inclination of the judiciary to align with societal or public welfare over individual economic freedoms, especially in contentious areas, mirrors Chilton and Versteeg's observations regarding courts' propensity to issue decisions that resonate with majoritarian preferences.

A. Implications of Aligned versus Nonaligned Interests

The study identifies a discernible pattern where businesses experiencing congruence between their objectives and third-party interests—spanning societal, consumer, or labor concerns—tend to fare better in legal challenges. This phenomenon underscores the judiciary's propensity to endorse economic freedoms when they are perceived to advance broader societal welfare.

A pertinent illustration of this dynamic is found in cases related to the medium or language of instruction in private schools. Here, the courts have recognized and upheld the right of parents to choose the medium of instruction for their children, aligning with the schools' prerogative to determine their instructional medium. This stance, adopted even in the face of expert opposition, exemplifies the judiciary's commitment to supporting decisions that resonate with the interests of broader communities, including the rights of parents and the autonomy of educational institutions.

B. Bar Dancers and Live Music Performers: A Closer Look

In Maharashtra, the legislation imposing restrictions on bar dancers was met with significant resistance, leading to legal challenges that brought both bar owners and bar dancers' unions to the forefront of a legal battle. The judiciary's approach in these cases was notably considerate of the bar dancers' dignity and their right to earn a living. This consideration was rooted in a clear understanding of the specific and tangible nature of the regulations, such as the mandatory installation of CCTV cameras, restrictions on the size of dance floors, and the segregation of different business areas. These regulations were seen as direct impediments to the dancers' professional autonomy and livelihood, prompting the Court to adopt a protective stance toward the dancers' fundamental rights and human dignity.

Conversely, the live music performance case in Karnataka depicted a scenario where the interests of live music performers—either as labor or consumers—were not directly represented before the Court. The regulatory restrictions in question were broad and somewhat ambiguous, lacking the specificity of the Maharashtra regulations but posing similar potential infringements on economic liberties. Despite this, the absence of explicit representation for performers meant that the adverse impacts of these restrictions remained underexplored in the judicial discourse, leading to a decision that did not critically address the rights and dignity of the performers.

The divergent outcomes in these cases underscore the critical role of third-party representation in legal proceedings concerning economic liberties. The Maharashtra judgments reflected a judiciary engaged with the nuanced interplay between regulatory measures and individual rights, especially when third-party interests were directly implicated and articulated. This engagement facilitated a judicial analysis that prioritized human dignity and fundamental rights over regulatory convenience.

In contrast, the Karnataka judgment reveals a gap in the judiciary's consideration of entrepreneurial and performer rights in the absence of direct representation. This gap suggests a judicial perspective that may inadvertently prioritize regulatory motives of safety and morality over the economic and expressive liberties of individuals, without a thorough examination of the broader implications for those affected by such regulations.

C. Dissenting Opinion and Populist Tendencies

The sole dissenting opinion challenging the majority's approach in the context of the 25 percent quota in private schools underscores a vital aspect of judicial decisionmaking: the balancing act between populist preferences and rigorous legal analysis.[21] This minority opinion, with its detailed examination of legislative history and precedents, starkly contrasts with majority rulings that lean toward populist stances. This divergence highlights a critical discourse on the sources of judicial legitimacy and credibility. Whereas the majority opinion prioritizes outcomes aligned with populist sentiments, the minority opinion champions a meticulous legal rationale, thereby questioning the premise that legitimacy stems solely from aligning with majoritarian views.

The scenario also hints at a potential oversight in legal strategy from those advocating against the quota system. A more nuanced approach, proposing alternative solutions (as lesser restrictive alternatives) that could address the concerns of all parties involved, might have shifted the judicial perspective. For instance, interpreting the nationalization of a quarter of seats in private schools as an opportunity for enhancing school choice, or suggesting voluntary reservations and direct cash transfers, could represent a form of innovative legal thinking. Such proposals not only challenge existing policy frameworks but also enrich the judicial discourse by presenting feasible options that reconcile economic freedoms with the goals of social welfare.

V. ΔIMPLICATIONS FOR PRACTITIONERS

The judiciary's aspiration to be portrayed as the protector of the downtrodden involves carefully balancing justice in favor of those less privileged while simultaneously maintaining a careful relationship with the state, avoiding direct conflict.

21. Society for Unaided Private Schools in Rajasthan v. Union of India (dissenting) (2012) 6 SCC 1.

Yet, this narrative unveils a paradox: a tendency to compromise its defense of liberty, including for businesses and entrepreneurs, particularly when such interests clash with those of the marginalized or environmental concerns.

For legal advocates, especially those focused on economic liberties, the challenge lies in integrating this judicial ethos into their narrative. Advocacy transforms into an intricate art, demanding a profound understanding of the judiciary's dual goals: safeguarding the marginalized while keeping a harmonious state relationship.

Lawyers are thus tasked with formulating arguments that resonate with the judiciary's social justice commitment, framing economic liberties as vital for societal well-being and beneficial to the marginalized. This involves not only amplifying those unheard voices in the courtroom but also presenting cases in a way that aligns with the judiciary's view of itself as champions of the underprivileged, demonstrating how economic freedoms can uplift the downtrodden without positioning the state as an adversary.

Strategically framing legal arguments is essential, emphasizing how economic liberties can promote dignity and inclusivity and enhance the lives of the marginalized. This strategy showcases how protecting these liberties aligns with the judiciary's wider social justice and equity goals, presenting economic freedom as a partner to the state's duties toward its citizens.

In this judicial landscape, advocating for economic liberties becomes a nuanced storytelling exercise. It involves recognizing the judiciary's desire to support the marginalized while subtly arguing that comprehensive social justice cannot be achieved without including economic freedom. This approach aims not just for favorable judicial outcomes but also for enriching judicial discourse with a deeper understanding of how economic liberties serve the marginalized, contributing to a broader effort to create a more equitable and just society.

CONCLUSION

This study delves into the Supreme Court of India's treatment of economic restrictions under Article 19(1)(g), revealing a discernible judicial inclination toward prioritizing societal welfare and third-party interests over individual business rights. It underscores a noticeable empathy for labor, consumer welfare, and broader societal concerns, often at the expense of business interests and the fundamental economic freedoms enshrined in

Article 19(1)(g). This tendency, coupled with a lack of depth in examining the second-order effects and the economic rationale behind regulations, suggests a judicial approach that tends toward superficial assessments of regulatory impacts. The findings indicate a variability in the Court's commitment to rigorous scrutiny, with a tendency to favor outcomes over a thorough evaluation of the means.

This nuanced understanding underscores an imperative for legal practitioners: to re-calibrate litigation strategies in favor of aligning arguments for economic freedom with demonstrable societal benefits and engaging effectively with third-party interests. It highlights the critical role of strategic framing in litigation, emphasizing the importance of weaving economic arguments into the broader fabric of societal welfare.

The broader implications of this research are significant, revealing a nuanced form of bias against a fundamental right that ostensibly stands on equal footing with other rights under Article 19. The study contributes to the academic discourse on economic liberties and judicial behavior, offering insights into the judiciary's apparent preferential treat-ment and the expanding net of restrictions on economic freedoms. It serves as a clarion call for future advocacy, charting potential strategies to navigate and counteract these judicial tendencies.

About the Cato Institute

Founded in 1977, the Cato Institute is a public policy research foundation dedicated to broadening the parameters of policy debate to allow consideration of more options that are consistent with the traditional American principles of limited government, individual liberty, and peace. To that end, the Institute strives to achieve greater involvement of the intelligent, concerned lay public in questions of policy and the proper role of government.

The Institute is named for *Cato's Letters*, libertarian pamphlets that were widely read in the American Colonies in the early 18th century and played a major role in laying the philosophical foundation for the American Revolution.

Despite the achievement of the nation's Founders, today virtually no aspect of life is free from government encroachment. A pervasive intolerance for individual rights is shown by government's arbitrary intrusions into private economic transactions and its disregard for civil liberties.

To counter that trend, the Cato Institute undertakes an extensive publications program that addresses the complete spectrum of policy issues. Books, monographs, and shorter studies are commissioned to examine the federal budget, Social Security, regulation, military spending, international trade, and myriad other issues.

In order to maintain its independence, the Cato Institute accepts no government funding. Contributions are received from foundations, corporations, and individuals, and other revenue is generated from the sale of publications. The Institute is a nonprofit, tax-exempt, educational foundation under Section 501(c)3 of the Internal Revenue Code.

Cato Institute
1000 Massachusetts Ave. NW
Washington, D.C. 20001
www.cato.org

www.ingramcontent.com/pod-product-compliance
Lightning Source LLC
Chambersburg PA
CBHW020206200326
41521CB00005BA/265